PENGUIN

ASSEMBLING ALICE

Mookie Katigbak-Lacuesta is the author of four poetry collections: *The Proxy Eros* (2008), *Burning Houses* (2013), *Hush Harbor* (2017), and *Eros Redux* (2019). She obtained an MFA from the New School University in 2004, and has since taught in major universities in Manila. Katigbak-Lacuesta has also co-edited various literary Filipino poetry anthologies for the Cordite Poetry Review and Vagabond Press. In 2019, she co-edited *The Achieve Of, The Mastery*, a survey of contemporary Philippine Poetry in English, with Dr. Gemino Abad.

Widely-awarded for her work in the Philippines, Katigbak-Lacuesta has also been the Filipino delegate to international literary festivals in Rotterdam, Medellín, San Francisco, Macau, and Kuala Lumpur. In 2015, she completed a writing residency for the International Writing Program at the University of Iowa.

Advance Praise for *Assembling Alice*

Acclaimed poet, Mookie Katigbak-Lacuesta, has outdone herself with this haunting and remarkable work of biofiction that not only straddles genres but cultures, history, and colonization as well. The starting point is a grandmother she never knew but reconstructs as a living-breathing family legend and survivor. In an age of forgetting, *Assembling Alice* is a powerful act of remembrance and unsentimental but loving awe.

–Robin Hemley, author of *Borderline Citizen*

Assembling Alice is more than just a portrait of a remarkable woman: it is a sharply-observed yet lyrically rendered depiction of an era: an age of secrets and scandals, of stifling social conventions and the people who flout them for good or bad, of gentility, hypocrisy and the horrors of war and gendered violence. It is above all a story of how the world breaks women -- and how women still muster the strength and spirit to rebuild themselves, their families, their nations. In the telling of this story, Mookie Katigbak-Lacuesta lends her distinct, indelible voice to the grandmother she has never met. But even as she does, she makes abundantly clear to us that her grandmother had a voice all her own.

–FH Batacan, author of *Smaller and Smaller Circles*

Assembling Alice

Mookie Katigbak-Lacuesta

PENGUIN BOOKS
An imprint of Penguin Random House

PENGUIN BOOKS

USA | Canada | UK | Ireland | Australia
New Zealand | India | South Africa | China | Southeast Asia

Penguin Books is part of the Penguin Random House group of companies
whose addresses can be found at global.penguinrandomhouse.com

Published by Penguin Random House SEA Pte Ltd
9, Changi South Street 3, Level 08-01,
Singapore 486361

First published in Penguin Books by Penguin Random House SEA 2021
Copyright © Mookie Katigbak-Lacuesta 2021

10 9 8 7 6 5 4 3 2 1

ISBN 9789814954105

www.penguin.sg

Table of Contents

v

For my grandmother Alice, and my mother Ana Maria.

This is a story inspired by historical people and events. Events narrated are based on oral tales told by Alice Feria and about Alice Feria by her contemporaries. As far as oral tradition goes, this book is a documentation of stories shared by the women in my family. Research situated these stories in their proper historical context. Where identities could not be properly verified given the passage of time and the availability of their precise characters, composite characters have been created and name changes have been applied to the narrative.

Part One

Baguio 1939-1940

The Stranger, 1939

He walks to the front lawn of the house dressed in a camisa de chino and trousers that barely lick his ankles. The topmost button of the crewneck shirt hurts the dip between his collarbones. He turns the button to the right and itches to flick it loose. He stops himself. Local men would have kept the button tight, whatever the weather. Strange to this place, he must not look out of place. If he cannot look like their men, he must appear to respect their ways.

He walks to the front lawn with the kind of purpose that clicks his heels but does not quite know why.

A large bird squawks overhead. The man takes this as a sign that this is not a good time to announce himself. He bounds across the street to his hiding groove: low fruit trees hedged around an unfinished cabin. He is lucky that the work on this log house has been stalled for weeks now. There are no workers or foremen in sight.

It is cool here in Baguio—cool, or cold, depending on the time of day. The long sleeves tenderly graze the goosebumps on his arms. When he rubs the wild rash under the camisa's warm cotton, the skin falls smooth almost suddenly.

He surveys the lawn roses: a subtle lavender he has never seen before: his only word for it is blue. He squares his shoulders as the house comes into fuller view. There are two gables—one nestled gently atop the front porch, and another forming a wider triangle above it. He sees the crooked path swerve gently to the front door. It is an amiable house with a long front porch and white windows with emerald green frames.

Once he finds himself there, he will not know quite what to do. He knows he is to introduce himself to the man of the house with only the few English words he knows. He knows he will have to sweep with his hands the reach of the garden; that he will have to proclaim in broad gestures that he has come to maintain an already well-kept lawn. He is not a sophisticated man but he knows the foolishness of this ruse.

He knows that the master of the house is there because parked in front of the gravel path is his midnight blue Studebaker Champion—its hood jutting at him like a barroom challenge. It's been rubbed to such a shine that he can't tell if the car is dark blue or black. The white wheels seem plump; seem to have mastered every swerve and bend of the road leading up to the City of Pines from somewhere so distant as Manila.

He knows that the man of the house does not live here, that this is the man's country cottage—a place he visits twice a month when he needs a short rest from the city. He knows that this man has a driver, a wife, a son, a daughter. He knows that the man is a distinguished lawyer from Manila.

He knows the lazy curl on the man's forehead by a picture in the brief. He knows the slow sag of dark circles under the man's eyes that seem to him more purplish than black—something the man was born with, perhaps, and not something high or low living—or both—had brought on him.

In the brief, the man had worn a black bowtie—meticulously drawn on each end, the right side dipping only half an inch below the left. Some small hurry perhaps worrying his mind to this small imperfection. His hairline recedes only on one side of his head, revealing an almost strangely stout forehead. There is the whisper of a moustache on either side of his mouth, dark wisps that never quite meet on the thick cleft between his nose and upper lip.

He expects the man to show up in this bowtie, and in a white suit. He knows this man's circle in Baguio: the driver Cardo, the cook Tentay, the wife Josephine, and the daughter Linang. Ages, respectively: thirty-five, fifty, forty-three, twenty-one. There is also a son, Macario, twenty-three, who he has never seen.

He watches as Cardo the driver hands a basket to the cook, Tentay. From the edge of the handled weave, he sees the long stems of carrots spill past the top of the rim. Cardo had driven Tentay here two days ago with the master's wife. He had deposited them and had driven back to what he assumed was Manila.

Before the master's arrival, only slow motions in the house: Tentay drawing the bedspread up in the Master's bedroom (rear left window), and then tucking the creases tightly under the mattress; Josephine in the kitchen (front left window) in front of Tentay discussing the contents of a book. Sometimes Josephine in the living room drawing back the floral curtains to reveal gingham loveseats to the right of the room, or a piano to the left.

He has noticed that Josephine is kind to Tentay, is spare with her orders, does not eat after six-o-clock in the evening. Past six these last two days, he has seen Josephine walk, glass in hand, among the roses in the garden. The glass, he has noted, is too small for wine or water—it is speckled with rough glass from middle to bottom. In the garden, she has brought the petals to her nose indulgently. He has not thought that roses had a particular scent to them, but they have brought upon Josephine's face a rapture he has never seen before. In her face, he has seen both perfume and thrill—in the ways her eyes close, in the way her shoulders arch gingerly.

Josephine reminds him of his mother, and he thinks—briefly—that he would suffer anything for her. *Come in,* he had imagined her saying, *come in from the cold, from the crickets in the cold.*

But the last of that dream was over already last night. He had woken to the fury and grumble of a car driving up the street. He had missed the man leaving the car, had missed the tender way the man had opened the left passenger seat to his daughter, Linang. He had seen Cardo the driver lift the basket for today's lunch to Tentay.

He had woken late, at noon, just as the sojourners from Manila inside the cottage are getting ready for lunch. He will have to act now because Manileños will want to take their siestas after lunch. The man of the house might just have been handed a whisky to take the edge off his journey from Manila. He might be in the first flush of good feelings. Now is the right time, he thinks to himself.

He stiffens his shoulders. He crosses the road, gives the Studebaker's long front length a gentle muss. He caresses the roses in the front lawn with his right hand. He is taking his time in seconds. If anyone is watching him from the windows, he must appear to love roses. That's enough, he thinks to himself, meaning this show which has seemed excessive to such a spare man. He walks the short length to the front door. He rings the bell. The man in the picture in the brief answers the door.

Yes? asks the man, not in the black bowtie or in the white suit he had anticipated—but in the very camisa de chino he himself is wearing.

Your garden, he tells the man. *I help.*

Where are you from? asks the man, turning his head to the right, his left eye squinting suspiciously at the interloper.

Japan, he answers. The man looks into his eyes.

Far from home, the man says.

No job home, he tells the man in the brief. *Then come to Philippines.*

What is your name? the man asks.

Haruki.

The man's eyes turn wistful. It dawns on him that this boy might be his son's age.

How can I help you then, Haruki?

I am gardener. Can help with roses.

Haruki, 1939

In this enclave of the very rich, I am embarrassed by the very rich. There is a war looming on the horizon, and still they bring out their best silver for breakfast. They ask me to clip the roses in the garden for their silver breakfast trays.

These are genteel people. These are people with homes in Manila and cottages in Baguio, one hundred and fifty miles north of, which is where you can find me now. Here an old American President had found a private haven within these meadows and pines. Here, his famous architect Burnham had transformed Baguio into a summer capital. You can tell these are American houses with their gables and stiff, aristocratic lines. A fetish for pillars. Well-kept lawns.

I know that they had wanted to name an army camp after one of their secretaries of state, John Hay, and that they had done so by seizing the land of one of the natives who sued them for his property. This did not stop them from building a country club where their ladies wore fashionable gowns every Saturday night, and where the gentlemen wore tweed.

Reports have it that the governor generals and secretaries sometimes dressed as 'tribesmen', and had drunkenly slapped their mouths, hallooing like Indians, or what they perceived as Indians.

How funny that it is in these civil eyes houses that you can find the most predatory American appetites, I have heard Callao saying to Linang. I write down the few words I know and stitch them together when I am alone. Funny, and house, and American. Civil eyes? Pred-a-tory.

When the two feel stifled indoors, they steal away to the garden.

It is here that Callao pours his whisky. When he is either very glad or very downcast, he lets Linang sip from his glass. And then the man talks. He talks of what he calls American civilization—when he says the last word, he scratches the air with the forefingers and middle fingers of his left and right hands simultaneously. He does this many times with the words, *civilization* and *democracy*. I do not know what he means by that, except maybe he is angry with these words every time they come after the word *American*. The daughter nods, puts in a word here and there, but mostly she listens.

Just like an American, though, Callao loves the cooler climate of Baguio, and the idea of a summer—if not capital— then place. His house is small compared to the American houses, but I understand that his house in Manila is practically a palace. Callao then must be a very rich and educated man. He is also a man who can speak many languages, for he speaks to the cook in their native tongue, Tagalog, and he speaks to his wife in Spanish, and he speaks to his daughter in English.

Cardo, the driver speaks to Callao in Tagalog, to Linang in halting English, and to Mrs Callao in halting Spanish. Cardo speaks to me in lingual semaphore. 'Cardo,' he says, patting his hand on his heart. 'Haruki,' I tell Cardo, patting my hand on my heart. *Alipores,* Cardo says, pointing to himself with a laugh. *Alipores,* Cardo says, pointing to Tentay with a sigh. *Amo,* the driver says, pointing to the Callaos when they greet each other at the front door. He nudges his head toward Linang when she breezes past us in the garden, *Bunso*, he says.

As the visits progress, and as I see them more and more: *mag-asawa,* Cardo says about the Callaos, *byuda,* Cardo says about Tentay, and *layaw*, Cardo says about Linang, *lumaki sa layaw.*

They are all very relieved and happy when Callao and the girl arrive, as though Manila were one long terrible burden, and their idea of paradise is still this American one. This meadow, these pines, this mountain.

I do not like the mountains having been born in O—.

My mother likes to say I was born during a storm, but my father once told me I was born in a time of calm—that the day I was born, he had set out with Sato and Torakiyo, his childhood friends and fellow fishermen, and that they had netted a beggar's bounty on their silver nets. For that kind of plenty, those would not have been stormy seas.

Further, my father told me that he and his friends would have taken that as an auspicious sign of my own bountiful and lucky life. No sooner had he drawn in his bounty, and moored his skiff to shore, then Izumi, my mother's younger sister would have told him that my mother had birthed me.

He had asked her if my first cry had been strong, and she would have told him that strong or not, it had been an angry first lungful of air. Did the child survive? He would have asked her, and she would have said she had never known any child more angry to be alive. That would have kept him going that odd mile home to his fisherman's house, would have eased his guilt for not being there at the exact moment of my birth. He would have walked briskly with the day's catch and not run home like his very life depended on it.

Why my mother told me I had been born during monsoon season would be anybody's guess. Perhaps she wanted me to know to myself that I was a survivor—that, at least, was her story. She did not tell me that I had come early, she told me that I was only too eager to enter the world. She did not tell me that the village's only midwife had been birthing the son of the village merchant who had been born at the right place, at the right time. She would only tell me, at five, that she had birthed me alone, that all the village midwife need have done is cut the cord that tied us together.

My mother did not raise me good and right—she did not raise me to be rich, she raised me to know how to survive. She did not raise me to be a general, she raised me to be a soldier. She raised me to know how to evade the envy of my peers and to know my station in life—to have just the right amount of luck to endear me to the gods, and love me to them with my helpless willingness. She raised me to fight a war; she did not raise me to clip roses.

When Callao and his family return to Manila, these are the things that occupy me during these waiting days. It is only a matter of time when the war will have repercussions here—that, at least, is the dispatch. For now, we must be cool and calm like my father.

Unlike my father, however, Callao always appears to be under a great burden when he arrives here from Manila. I do not care about the capital city, and I barely know Manila. Once I caught a sunset there, and it dipped like the sun in my flag. A big orange globe dipping down Manila Bay, round as an egg yolk. It is only this bright red I see when everyone else swears that as the sun sets, the bay takes on other lush colours, as if the very air were a prism transforming a singular glow into lush unexpected tones of blue and yellow, and then damask. I do not see those colours except in Callao's garden; on that one day out of every month that I allow myself to think of my mother and father.

Haruki, 1939

When the lawyer brings his daughter Linang up to the summer cottage, nothing stirs in me.

She is pleasant enough to look at but hers is not a comely face. It is a boyish one that would have suited her best as a man. As a woman, it is severe. Her hair is sheared to a length below her ears, grazing her chin. I know this is the popular way. We have the same shade of skin now that I have been spending most of my days outdoors in the garden. Her nose is hawk-like like her father's but her eyes are shaped like quarter moons, the irises dark as her hair.

Callao has brought her three times now to his cottage in Baguio since the beginning of my time here. She is dressed, as always, in the American style: a patterned dress cinched at the waist, the hemline falling to just below the calf. Sometimes it is a plaid dress, sometimes it is striped or floral. I realize now that no matter how well or how little I like the pattern, Linang can wear anything well. Her silhouette is slim. Her limbs are long.

Callao parades her as fathers do their daughters during Shichi-Go-San, buying them the most expensive kimonos, and offering auspicious gifts in shrines around the country. I think of those kimonos when I see Linang leave the car and leap toward the porch to her mother. I think of Callao looking at Linang as though she were a little girl who had tied her obi by herself for the first time.

Sometimes Linang looks at me and wrinkles her nose. Other times, she pretends I am not there. In these ways I know the depth of her disdain, for I am neither the poor servants who have raised her, but I *am* a kind of servant, tending her father's garden.

* * *

Mrs Callao has come two days ahead to prepare for her family. She has been working with Tentay about this weekend's menu, but her manner has been terse and her voice edgy. It is the first time I have seen her bothered.

Since almost the minute Mrs Callao arrives, Tentay and her kitchen have been stewing with various smells—beef and vegetables, and what I'm hazarding are bananas, from the cloying, sweet smell. Tentay has been hard at work since Mrs Callao's arrival. Strange things have simmered in pans, whiffs declare themselves as stewed vegetables, as beef; the sizzle on a pan means pork.

I do not feel sorry for myself that all I have is my tin of rice. When Tentay feels especially generous, she shares small bits of fish with me from the marketplace. She gives me a companionable lonely look, not knowing that this fish fills me—it reminds me of home.

There were days back home when there was nothing but rice; and then days when there wasn't even that. Those days were the days I looked forward to most in my younger life because those days were the days when my mother told me stories.

She told me the story of the farmer's son who only wanted to be a samurai. That he forsook his home, wife, and child, to join Tokugawa's army. That he spent a year's wages on the samurai uniform he could find at a kiosk in a marketplace that sold pottery and kimonos. Like pottery and some of the shiny kimonos, the uniform seemed almost ornamental. To see him decked out in the ensemble of only the basic helmet, mask, and armor of a samurai, you would have seen a man who looked like a farmer but walked like a general.

Somewhere, he had beheaded the enemy's most prized general, and had affixed himself to the rear of Tokugawa's army. He is cheered on; he is called a hero. So much a hero, in fact, that he is brought to the very best brothel in the land. There he finds his wife, forced into kept womanhood, by his hasty abandonment.

* * *

When she does not have fish enough for the both of us, Tentay slides her fingers down the small length of fish and dips them, I know, into my rice. This kind gesture makes me think of lean times back home, father's spare catch, mother's downturned face.

* * *

The samurai spends one last amorous evening with his wife, and leaves with his army at daybreak. I have always felt that he made the right decision. Since I heard the tale, I have always taken it to mean how love of one's country is the most sublime expression of love, that romantic or filial or conjugal love must either hold sway to a man's ambition, or falter and fade as collateral damage. I had told my mother this once, and she had slapped my face. *You are getting it all wrong,* she had told me, *you are getting it all wrong.*

Folk Beliefs, 1939

This time, the Studebaker is almost full. Haruki sees another figure in the backseat beside Linang. This time Callao sits in the passenger seat. There again is the squawk of that terrible bird. Haruki starts. He glances up at an overcast sky but the bird has already flown away.

Haruki is distracted, is sure now more than ever that it will be a terrible day, that it will be a terrible weekend—the tenor of which had been set first by Mrs Callao's unforgiving temper, and now this pernicious bird, and then the fact of a stranger in Callao's Studebaker.

Linang exits excitedly from the right side of the car. Cardo opens the left back door. Haruki does not know who to look at first: Linang, or Callao, or the guest. There is a strange flurry to his senses—all seem to be conversing with him at the same time. There is the stranger exiting the car, but there is also Linang shrieking, 'Mama! Mama!' 'Mama,' Haruki hears her, again, 'Alice has finally agreed to join us!'

This is the first time anyone new has been brought to the cottage since Haruki started watching it, first from across the street and then now up close. This will be a new development in the report, Haruki thinks to himself. He does not like developments or the unravelling of a story he has stitched together so meticulously. Most of the time, this is what developments do—they undo stories it takes months to carefully craft.

There, alighting, is the most suspicious thing Haruki has ever seen. *It* has made the sky overcast. Haruki thinks *it* because he cannot tell yet if it is a woman or a man. Haruki thinks the weather was sunny minutes ago but now it might rain. As *it* pulls into view, striding toward him—*him!*—and not the house or the hosts beyond as Linang has always done, Haruki sees it is a *her*.

She is dressed like Linang: loose dress, tight waist, blousy sleeves. Haruki amends his mind: even as she is dressed like Linang, she is not like Linang—she has light hair and fair skin. When she sees Haruki, her shoulders do not tense. She gives him a smile. 'How do you do?' she asks. It—she—extends her right hand to him.

Haruki gives her a bewildered look. 'How do you do?' she asks again. And then he remembers himself. He wipes his right hand on his soiled camisa. 'Haruki,' he says, patting his heart. And then to address her first and only question, and one that she has had to ask twice: 'Haruki is fine.'

'It's nice to meet you, Haruki. My name is Alice.'

She shakes his hand and then withdraws it almost too soon. She had seen a stranger first, and now she sees a servant. Her friendliness turns vague. She smiles shyly at Haruki and then briskly walks to the front door where Linang, Mr Callao and Mrs Callao are waiting. Haruki hears her say, 'What a strange man,' to Mrs Callao, kissing her left cheek and her right. Mrs Callao purrs a discreet assent. 'Was it a long trip, darling?' Mrs Callao asks her.

'Oh, so very long, *tita*.'

'Poor dear,' says Mrs Callao. 'Come into the house, I'll show you to your room.'

Haruki looks at the hem of his dirty shirt, at the smear of mud above it. He is his mother's dear, he thinks to himself, but he feels suddenly very unimportant. He doesn't know what it is about the girl that makes him feel poor even as he has always known it. And why it has suddenly started raining. Or why the sun is out at the same time it is raining.

Cardo sidles up to where Haruki stares blankly at the sky. 'A *tikbalang* must be getting married,' Cardo says. Haruki shakes his head, indicates he doesn't know what Cardo means. He has never felt so confused at something Cardo has said, even now that Cardo is a familiar, and even now that he and Cardo understand each other without having to understand exactly what the other is saying.

He misses Cardo's explanation that a *tikbalang* is a Filipino creature with a horse's head and a man's body. He misses Cardo's elaboration that it is a common folk belief that when rain and sun happen at the same time such a creature is getting married, and that the weather is as confused as the creature is at the sum of his parts. Which is a pity because this is a story Haruki would have been able to relate to at this moment—his body feels like it is turning against him, and he has never felt so discombobulated; his head feels heavy but his torso seems now so very small, as though he were staring at his body from outside it, or from a far height, or through eyes so supernatural, they might as well be stars.

Linang

I am my mother's daughter but it should have been Alice.

Imagine all the elegant mistakes in that one phrase. Should have been. Three words that begin with a human wish and end with disappointment. Call it the million ways the universe can intercept a wish. Call it the many ways a human wish can land an inch away from God's ear.

I was not the daughter my mother wished for, but I was the one she had. I was the one she fought for in 1937 when women won the right to vote in the Philippines after a decade of mobilization among her *kumadres*, and the quick and tender wheedling of their husbands in congress. I was the argument against statesmen who declared that the women's vote would undermine the man of the house by giving his wife the same rights.

Let me be the first to tell you, I was not raised in a suffering household. Vote or no, my life would not have varied much or steered too far from its natural course. And so, my mother's struggle had seemed immaterial to the lives we led in Manila. My mother brought the news home to me, but it happened that Alice had been with me that day, and only one of us had received the news rapturously. Only one of us had seemed to care for what mama had called The Cause. This cause being mama's 'feminist' project as part of the *Asociación Feminista*. It was Alice who had squealed with glee, and it was she who had thanked my mother for her 'contributions to the cause.'

It was my belief then—as it is now—that Alice didn't so much as want my mother's vote as she wanted my mother's approval. She does not know that that kind of approval is such a small, pious, domestic thing.

My father says that these are German times in the world, just as sure as these are American times in the Philippines. When he is on his third glass of whisky, he admits he is afraid that Japanese times are in place in the world and that they are coming to the Philippines. When Alice has dinner with us, and Papa talks to us in the same way he talks to his *kumpares*, she looks at him, bright-eyed with admiration. This look had so irked me—he was, after all, *my* papa and not hers—until I understood the meaning of that look. She looks around and sees a unit she must not see in her own home—a man, his wife, their son and daughter. When her eyes assess the table, turning from my father, to my mother, to Macario, and then to me, I realize that it isn't really my father she is enthralled by, it is the idea of a family unit.

All Alice has is a spinster aunt from the provinces who has inherited her brother's unwanted child. She has tried to hide her provenance from me, but I belong to Manila society, a league of professional gossip-mongers who have been prone all their colonial lives, not to truth, but to Chinese whispers. When I hear gossip from my mother that Alice is highborn, and comes from sugar money, and then I hear from my cousin Trinidad that Alice is the bastard child of a rich *haciendero* and a lowly Mestiza nurse from Bukidnon, somewhere there is the truth.

Somewhere in between is always the truth. My mother has time and again implored me to be Christian with Alice, but I do not know if I can forbear her any longer—as a Christian, or as simply myself, Linang Callao.

Even now, two years after we have been granted the vote, how cross, how labourious still is Alice when she talks of the female cause to my mother. Here we are, having a perfectly pleasant dinner and still the girl prattles on as if we are decades away from winning our vote. My mood shifts from indulgence to frustration in a short minute.

Politically, I am happy to defer to papa and often recycle his views during cocktail parties (to great success, I might add). It is my papa and his *kumpares* who speak of the larger politics almost every night in their secret places. There my father, the good lawyer, talks to his contemporaries of the Filipino cause, and who to install in power, and how to become a republic. There my father, the good lawyer speaks to his *kumpares* who scoffed at the word commonwealth, but who wink at the words *Asociacion Feminista*, except when they are with their wives. As you can tell, my father is not a resting man.

As a child, I used to watch the long curls of his cigarette drift into wisps of air, over and over; a long, lethargic nimbus of smoke that drifted with me into my short afternoon nap. Those days, I had my father for one hour, and that one hour had always seemed as holy as Sunday.

These days I do not have him at all.

These days, entire days go by that I do not see Papa. When I have his full attention is here in Baguio. When he, as in days gone by, gives us books to read during the day, so that we can discuss them—often headlong and passionately—into the night.

We did well the first time with *Madame Bovary*. But then Papa committed the eternal mistake of giving both me and Alice

Gone with the Wind. Mama had hated the book, but papa had said that it was the novel that had swept America by storm this past half decade. Last month, Alice and I had seen the movie version at a matinee at the Zen theater in Manila. Alice had only said that it was a rapturous, sad little romance. She had never seemed more like a ninny, to quote Scarlett O' Hara herself. When I returned home, Papa had said that I would do well, someday, to read the book, and not just watch the movie. Shortly after, he had brought home a book I first mistook as an encyclopedia. Mitchell's American classic weighs about as much as mama's Chinese Double Happiness vase, and so I roll my eyes when Papa slips the tome into my hand.

Papa does not have much time for reading these days, even as he is the most well-read man I know. That he appears to know the entire plot and can voice his own thoughts about the civil war—a war, he says, not unlike the defection of oligarchs from The Old President's 'tribe' in the Philippines at the turn of the century—is a magnificent display of Filipino showmanship.

These days, he reads only brief articles about *en vogue* books, enough to discuss them during cocktail parties, to seem worldly, and modern, and topical. 'My lexicon's as long as a cocktail party,' papa used to say in jest. When he is with The President, The President laughs. 'Callao, everyone knows your lexicon is as long as the bible,' he says.

It is an accomplishment to him to know what novel his daughter should read so that she keeps ahead of his friends' daughters. I hear him whisper to mama how polished I am—if only, he says, I can know Tagalog as well as I know English or the Western canon.

Of course, Alice hadn't enjoyed the epic novel after reading *Uncle Tom's Cabin*; she had seen it as a novel of slavery, and cunning white enterprise. She had gone on about how white prosperity had rested on the backs of slaves. I, however, had seen it as a novel of survival. I saw myself as its sharp-tongued heroine. I knew I was in for the long haul with that opening line alone. *Scarlett O' Hara was not beautiful*, which is perhaps the only attribute that distinguishes me from her. And still, having neither beauty nor particular education, she had survived a war and the total annihilation of her childhood. Had not just survived, in fact, the girl had actually thrived.

I suppose Alice had felt especially passionate about the book, seeing as her own father's family in the provinces rested on the same feudal systems; and while the workers who tilled her father's fields were not slaves, they might as well have been, given their meagre wages and their ramshackle lives. Thanks largely to their toil, her father had nested in his stone house every day, secure in the knowledge that his children would be prosperous. How many times, Alice says, had he hitched up his latest child to his arm to overlook, past open *capiz* windows, hectares upon hectares of sugarcane, and had said *one day, this will be yours*. Such words he would never say to Alice.

When mama had looked rapturously at her during dinner, Papa gave me a long, conspiratorial, bittersweet smile. I know I had done the proper critique when we both brought our strong assessments over dinner that evening. Alice had said something to the effect that to pertain to Southern men as cavaliers was an uneducated assessment. Henceforth, she bemoaned their arrogance as the arrogance of a passel of children who passed themselves off as men. 'Passel' being a word I know Alice also learned from Mitchell's book herself; the author has her heroine say it in one of the first chapters. It had seemed to me to be pretentious to know such an American word and to passionately, effortlessly, breathe it into a cool Filipino night, into the eardrum of my coolly Filipino and impressionable father, who looked to be lauding a young Filipina's easy usage of the American vernacular.

I had spoken, clearly, I felt, about how to be a true heroine—and a true *feminista*. This last word had won a chuckle from my mother, who pretended to cough into her napkin. 'And how is Scarlett O'Hara a feminist, *mi hija*?' My mother had asked me. 'Well, she knew how to survive, didn't she?' Mama had only looked at me indulgently. *Indulgently*. I tried another tack. 'She built her own lumber business just after the war, didn't she?' 'Yes, dear,' said Alice. 'But on the backs of underpaid convicts, who she chose as workers.' Mother had then looked rapturously upon her again. Father had said, for the first time ever in my life, a word against me: 'Well, she does have a point, doesn't she, Linang?' A sad, but amused look in his eyes. 'Light my cigarette, won't you, dear,' he says, shucking a stick from his pack of Parliaments.

Tonight, in our shared bed, Alice is all atonement and apology. 'But there is nothing to apologize for, *dear*,' I say, affecting mother's word, mother's tone. Alice's face has such a worried, beseeching look upon it; so brown are her eyes at this moment, so softened by candlelight, I feel the old envy start in me. Compounded with the knowledge that I had lost tonight's debate—I do not *discuss* I *debate*—my threadbare composure remembers me to myself, tells me exactly what I need to hear: that between me and Alice, I am by far the more privileged one. The epiphany comes in the nick of time, just as the envy I feel threatens to turn into hate.

Haruki, 1940

To see Callao's gentle eyes now, you would not have thought that he had written in his youth a contentious essay against the Americans called *Buwitre*. This essay had been published in a local anti-American paper called *El Nuevo Sol* where public intellectuals served as directors, editors, and writers.

Callao had alluded then to Dean Worcester, secretary of the insular government of the Philippines, as a vulture. Or so Worcester had thought. Worcester, in his position, had full control of the city slaughterhouses. It was alleged, in Callao's essay, that the American had used his position to profit from the sale of cattle meat. In the same essay, it was also alleged that the American had researched on an ethnic tribe in Benguet—a place situated in the same region as Baguio—to seek out gold sources. Finding out that source, Callao alleged—or rather Worcester had alleged Callao had alleged—had given Worcester great wealth.

From time to time, when I see Callao glance at me from the window of the living room, the article I keep feels heavy in my pocket. In my brief, I wonder if something has been lost in translation, from Spanish to English to Japanese. The article seems less like an editorial to me and more like poetry.

There are birds of prey, Callao had written, *that unlike the proud eagle, swoop down on the vulnerable, the poor and the weak. They swoop down on the poor tribes of our high mountains to 'civilize' them—in truth, they mean only to spy on their sources of gold and wealth. They mean only to acquire this wealth for themselves. These vultures only think of how to make their fortunes vaster.*

I warn you that there are powerful men among us. These are men who act as high and mighty as the eagle, but are in truth, only swooping vultures; they are only ever birds of prey.

No mention of the name Worcester, but Worcester had sued Callao for libel. The man would have lost all his wealth and prestige had then-Governor General Harrison not granted him pardon. This signalled the end of Callao as a writer, but had won him such favor with the Commonwealth President, that the Filipino leader had named him his Secretary.

At least, this is the official story of Callao's political promotion. The unofficial story is something I first heard from Cardo and then heard again from Mrs Callao, recounting the story to Alice in the garden.

Mrs Callao says that Callao grew up like a younger brother to the President and that the president had appointed Callao to his cabinet because of their friendship.

During a luncheon at the Polo Club with the American General MacArthur, Callao had stood in the President's entourage behind him as one among a small cadre of oligarchs who called themselves *nacionalistas*. They were a small group of rich back-slappers and Callao, who was rich but who was not a back-slapper, and whose presence at the luncheon was meant to prove the President's importance to MacArthur.

The President had been pleased that he had been allowed entry into the Polo Club—one of the few times he had been granted grudging entry into the largely American grounds.

This had given his bearing a certain stunted dignity and given his face an unattractive jut in the chin and a tight purse in the lips. 'Imagine that Alice,' Mrs Callao had said. 'An unattractive moment for the handsomest man in the Philippines.'

During the aperitif, he had let one rip, or at least Callao had told his wife. It was the roiling kind of air that smelled of horse manure and grass for brisk but long seconds. MacArthur, Callao said, had looked amused and had cleared his throat, knowing that the president had just passed the most awesome and low-class gas in all of Luzon.

With that one passing, MacArthur would have been convinced that all Filipino leaders were heathen and as common as American farm boys. Or so the President had thought.

The Polo Club had allowed Filipinos entry into their grand halls not long before that day.

It had taken some effort on MacArthur's part to convince the proprietor Forbes that there were Filipino folk who could be afforded entry into these hallowed horse grounds, and that the Filipino gentry deserved to be here as much as any American. The President had held himself as a proud example. Only, here was his undeniable foul air, and not even during the main course at that, only appetizers.

He had so wanted to prove himself to this soldier and *Americano*, that Callao said the good man had reddened to a ripe flush. MacArthur had so undeniably caught on that the foul source had been the president himself, that he had suppressed a chuckle. The President had only cleared his throat like a proper showman and made it abundantly clear that he was waiting on one the five men behind him to take the blame. No one but

Callao had had the balls to do so. 'Excuse me, Mr President,' he had said. And just like that, Callao was promoted to Presidential Secretary.

This bond between Callao and the most powerful Filipino today, you who I address, friend or foe, is why I find myself here.

Agony in the Garden, 1940

When Alice is in Baguio, she and Linang have breakfast in the garden on wrought iron chairs that face each other across an identical table with a glass top. Haruki knows that whatever they leave over on their plates will be Tentay's breakfast this morning, and by extension, his. Today, breakfast consists of round, caramelized sausages and rice fried in garlic. They will top off the meal, Haruki sees, with strawberries in a bowl of sugared milk. This will not be part of his breakfast.

Each girl wears a matching set of sleepwear—cotton trousers with a matching top cinched at the waist with a sash. Linang wears a robe on top of her apricot set while Alice wears a shawl over her blue one. They sit in a shroud of warm sunlight and young laughter. Haruki feels for the first time like the world is a garden—a natural arrangement of stones and sunlight. A composition of flowers and hedges. An order of appetites.

Did you see the way Ding looked at me at the dance, Alice?

Yes, he seems very smitten, Linang.

It is the first time Haruki has heard the name Ding, which does not sound grand like *Juan,* Callao's first name, or *Josephine,* his wife's. It does not sound elegant like *Alice,* but it sounds like a pet name like *Linang.* A pat on the cheek, a kiss in the hair. A dotage.

I mean those eyes, Alice.

You mean 'that physique,' Linang.

Again, young laughter.

I mean, it's enough for me to forget myself, Alice.

Haruki's solemn mouth draws to a smile. It seems to him that Linang has a weakness after all.

If only he didn't love basketball so much. Linang says, her mood suddenly solemn.

If only he learned how to fence like Macario, Linang continues.

Macario Callao, twenty-three years old, the only Callao boy, Haruki thinks.

Not everyone can be like Macario, Linang.

Do you fancy him, Alice—I mean, not Ding, but Macario?

Haruki sees Alice blush.

Goodness, no, Linang.

Really, he and Macario are such opposites, Alice. I don't know how they became friends.

They do go to the same school, Linang. Alice laughs.

Haruki pulls on the silver lever of his garden rose, thinks how like a gun it is. He remembers suddenly what his first gun felt like, remembers how he had missed his first target by aiming dead centre, how his captain once said that if one wanted to shoot at another man's heart, one would have to aim at a button directly below it, and only then hit his mark more precisely than if he had aimed at the heart itself. The captain had said to him, *you want to aim over there to get over here.*

For a reason he cannot explain to himself, this is how the conversation between Linang and Alice has begun to feel: slant, not straight. *But how,* Haruki thinks to himself, *can one ever really hit a target without aiming directly at it?*

When Linang mentions Macario's name, Alice's eyes do not shine. When Linang mentions Ding, Alice cannot look into her eyes.

Linang, 1940

All my modern rhetoric dissolves when I think of my brother's closest *kumpare*, Ding Obordo.

Ding who occupies himself with an American sport called basketball. It has seemed to me such a basic pursuit when one considers that Macario grew up on fencing and chess. How hard is it, after all, to shoot a ball through a basket. To jump up with all your strength and height and shoot a ball through a netted hoop? Tentay, our cook, has known such skill, coming home from the market. You can be sure she has come brandishing nothing so common as a rubber ball, but with the week's essentials: beef and chicken, and *pechay*, and potatoes and carrots. There, you have it; two kinds of baskets, one essential, and one a pastime. The latter must be such a sketchy one that when one asks oneself what the American sport is, the answer is clear and singular. It is not basketball. It is such a non-sport that the Americans back home still cleave to their baseball. Papa says that it is just like the Americans to treat the Philippines like a laboratory of sorts; a laboratory of colonization, and even a laboratory of sports: that they want to see if the sport takes here before they even try it on their home turf. Such proclamations have made me second-guess myself: Do I want to bring home the unwitting master of the most basic sport known to mankind?

And yet. And yet, Ding. Five foot nine. Brown skin. Black hair. White smile. American in wile and wit. Ding who thinks he is *au fait* with all matters American. This knowledge makes me regard him with an almost motherly tenderness.

The first time I had seen him at the games with Macario, however, I did not have such motherly feelings. I did not see a Filipino who loved Americans, all I saw was the body of a young Greek hero. It was Rodin's bronze.

It had given me a strange warmth the first time I had seen him in the flush of that Padre Faura sunset in the university he shared with my brother. But then my inner mind had given me a strange poetry. I had been watching him many afternoons, passively at first, and then with more and more rapt attention. As soon as my eye had drawn to his form tenderly—as soon as I had the notion that there was nothing I wanted more in this life than to be Ding's bride, a strange line of poetry had drifted up and out from the ether. I knew it, and I hated it. It was Rilke. *You must change your life.*

The thought had come up casually, dispassionately, when I had imagined our lengthy, much-attended wedding at the Ermita Church. When I saw in my mind's eye, Mama's wedding *mantilla* and sapphire art deco earrings. When I imagined by the altar Ding's tears, and Papa hiding his, leading me into Ding's arms, pressing my hand into his. That life, that inner, imagined life. And then that Rilke quote suddenly drifting up and outward as if from the very air itself, telling me to revise even my interior mind, my one pure float of a dream. *Change,* said a voice I have since learned to quell.

When she visits me during slow afternoons, I tell Alice that one day I will marry Ding, and that our children will resemble mama in skin tone, and eye colour, and nose. That these traits may have skipped a generation, but my children will always be known as *whiteys*—to my father's *chagrin,* and my mother's pride. I do not know why it is that when I think of utter, complete happiness, it almost always means my mother's approval, and not my father's—I suppose it is only because my mother has always been so terribly hard to win over, and my father has been won over from the start.

At light's out, I tell Alice that I think I shall marry Ding before too long. He is in my house too much these days to be appropriate; and after all, we are both of marrying age. I ask her if she thinks Ding and I are a match. She looks at me, askance. Her thoughts war in her, I know, because Alice's default answer is *yes*. She cannot even give such a simple, yielding word.

I tell her that someday soon, I must explain my desire for Ding to Macario, and if all goes well, eventually to my mother and father. *Is he a match, Alice?* I ask again, impatiently this time. Alice remains silent, answers after a beat, *only time can tell, Linang.*

Nobility obliges, I hear my mother's voice in my head, when I most want to lash out at Alice.

Noblesse oblige, I whisper in the half-dark. 'What, darling?' asks Alice. 'Nothing, darling,' I answer. 'Nothing.'

Job's Tears, 1940

In truth, apart from the allegations that Worcester had exploited indigenous tribes from Benguet to learn more about their gold sources, the last straw that had prompted Callao to finally write *Buwitre* was a picture of a young Igorot girl that Worcester had taken.

A zoologist before he was an administrator, Worcester had taken photos of indigenous tribes up north, and had labelled the pictures as a seemingly objective scientist. These photos were designed as Worcester's ethnographic documentary, but Callao does not think that this photograph is a faithful depiction of the girl's ethnicity racially or culturally. The picture Callao had seen had been labelled: 'Bontoc Igorot girl, type 13. Full length, front view, nude,' as though she were some species of bird or flora.

The young girl does not look directly at the camera and had fixed her gaze, in fact, to the middle distance beyond it. Her hands modestly hide her sex. The only thing that she wears is a belt made of bark fibre, embellished with seeds. Callao had wondered if the young girl had actually consented to having her photograph taken nude, as Worcester had alleged. Worcester had further alleged that Bontoc women wore leaf skirts as they worked, so as not to smear their clothes. Callao doubts that this is so, but even if it were true, the woman in the photo does not wear the leaf skirt—the clothing can be found elsewhere in the photo. It is clear to Callao that the American had coerced the girl into removing what he alleges are her work clothes.

For a reason very clear to someone as politically-minded as Callao is, Worcester had depicted Filipinos as savages, following the nakedness of their northern tribes. It is clear to Callao that Worcester has done this to depict Filipinos as an uncivilized people who needed the civilization and education of their American colonizers. Worcester had never depicted Christianized people, or the Tagalogs to whom Callao belongs. Callao believes that the only pictures of Tagalogs that Worcester has produced up to this point have been photos of Filipino prostitutes in brothels in Manila.

The thought that Worcester used his background as a zoologist to depict but one cultural reality in the Philippines, sometimes using such coercive methods as have awed members of this tribe to remove their clothing, arguably against their will, as in the case of this Igorot girl—had so enraged Callao that he had found himself, one night, writing the article feverishly.

Some hours after he had penned his impassioned words, he had shown the article to the editor of El Nuevo Sol, who had agreed to publish the article on the front page of the paper. The editor had asked what had prompted such a poorly-disguised account of Worcester, and Callao had asked him if he had seen the photo of the young Igorot girl. The editor had of course seen it. 'A bit of trivia,' he had told Callao, 'but do you know what the bark used as the Igorot girl's belt is?' Callao had told him that he had no clue. 'It's something biblical—which is ironic given that Worcester had photographed non-Christian people.' 'Tell me,' Callao had said. 'It's called Job's tears.' The two had laughed. 'The joke's on Worcester then,' Callao had had told him, 'it appears even their clothing is more civilized than he is.'

For Callao, the essay was his version of an ethnographic photo. Only his subject was not a tribe. It was Worcester himself. It was his version of labelling his subject the way Worcester had labelled his. It was a long prose version of a species known as 'Worcester', a way of capturing him as naked as the Igorot girl. It was a Filipino rendering of what he could have called—had he been a photographer, and had this been a photograph and not an article—'Worcester, type 1, white torso, full length, front view, nude.'

Because he was a writer and not a photographer, he had wanted to capture Worcester with his words. He had also wanted to depict the American in terms Worcester would have understood as a zoologist. Buwitre, he had called him. Bald-faced vulture.

More than ten years after the article has been written, Callao finds himself in his Baguio garden watching his daughter Linang, and her friend Alice. They are tormenting the gardener by using his own water hose against him. Despite his pleas, Callao sees that the gardener cannot hide his pleasure—he is a young boy after all. 'No Ms Linang, no Ms Alice, you must not water me so,' the young man says. 'Just pretend we are you, and you are the roses,' Alice says. Linang laughs. 'You are Alice's rose, Haruki,' she says. Callao sees the boy look at Alice and then run away, moving in almost formal, fast strides. *Like a soldier*, Callao thinks to himself.

Haruki, 1940

I have told you that I am not an educated man—that I am a mere fisherman's child. You might argue that it is of no importance that one is educated for as long as one is a good man. I would not even think I was a good man, but when I see Alice and her kind eyes, she makes me want to be good.

My father was a survivor. As such he had no room in his life for poetry—which is not to say that my father did not possess any notions of beauty. He, too, taught me about beauty in his small but important way.

Make no mistake, I am a soldier through and through. I do not think that soldiering means doing a poet's job. Had I been given the choice to be either poet or soldier, I would still choose to be a soldier, even if one is both these days. For to die for one's country is poetic: I am prepared to die for my country as a soldier. I have no illusions about where my loyalties lie. I would forsake each and every one of these Filipinos—even Callao himself who has been nothing but kind to me. I would forsake them all. Except Alice. She brings out quite another

Haruki. And the Haruki she brings out—to my amazement and frustration—is a poet, not a soldier.

My father only had four good things in his life, or so he proclaimed—he had his wife, his child, the high seas—and his uncommon fisherman's fixation with a poet called Bashō.

'Quietly, quietly/ yellow mountain roses fall—/ sound of the rapids.'

That was the one poem my father taught me. And that poem had seemed to me to be emblematic of what it means to be human. To long for something quietly. The way I long for Alice.

My father had never been to the mountains. He had lived all his life by the sea. I know that it was his one true dream to visit our country's mountains. But this was not to be.

My father died the year I turned fifteen. The sun was high that day, so my mother says. So high that my father and Torakiyo had tried their luck and sailed out to sea. Before he left, my mother had told me, my father had said he had a feeling that that day would be the day his fortune would be reversed. So glad was his delight that day that my mother had believed him.

It had been years since I last saw my father and my mother joined in a kiss, but that morning my mother had met his mouth so joyfully with hers; so much had she believed in the dream that I had believe it, too.

I had believed so much in my father's dream that I had already imagined him a wealthy man. I had believed that he would end his day in the marketplace buying that kimono from a kiosk for my mother. I had already imagined my father bringing the cloth home to my mother. I had already imagined my mother's delight—how she would wrap the obi around her waist, how she would wear her hair up for the first time in years for my father.

I had already imagined how we would feast that night. Mother had already boiled rice—had already procured from Torakiyo's mother a proper vase of sake.

And then that noon storm. And then the fact of Torakiyo and my father never arriving.

We had thought them marooned on some island, making their way home after the storm had cleared. And then days passed, and then weeks. And then we knew for certain what had become of them.

We had never recovered my father's body, or Torakiyo's. My father's boat had never washed ashore. My mother remained a widow ever after. It was through her widowhood that I knew that despite their differences, my mother had loved my father.

I may have already told you this but I will tell you again: every useful thing I knew in life, I learned from my mother. Every useless thing, I had learned from my father. But we hardly ever remember the useful things. I hardly remember what I learned from my mother, except how to want to be a soldier. But I remember every useless thing my father taught me.

It is a supreme irony now that I find myself on a mountain tending roses—just like that Bashō poem. I would like to believe that I am living my father's dream. He continues through me, and whatever I make of my life. Through me, he cannot die.

I am writing a haiku in Callao's garden when Alice finds me. I have no scroll or pen. I am writing in pencil, on the back of the grocery list Mrs Callao has given Tentay. I am thinking of the proper cutting word for a haiku—for a haiku must have a proper cutting word. In Bashō's it is 'quietly' in the first line. That is the *kireji*.

My kireji, it just so happens, is 'father.'

Father, father/

Now I do not know how the poem proceeds. I know that I must make a seasonal reference for this to be a proper haiku. But I am at a loss.

Father, father/

I try.

It is always Spring/

Alright.

It is at this line that Alice finds me in the garden.

'What are you writing, Haruki?'

I explain to her, in my broken English, that I am writing a Japanese poem—that I am having trouble finding the last line. I tell her that I cannot reconcile my *kireji* and *kijo,* my line for the seasons. She understands. Alice always understands. I tell her in my rough English, what those first two lines are.

'The way I see it, Haruki,' she starts, 'the third line must connect the previous two lines somehow.' She studies my lines.

Father, Father,

It is always Spring

'It seems to me to be about how you associate spring with your father,' she says. 'And so you must reconcile both, somehow, in the third line. 'Let me think on it, Haruki—will you allow me this?'

Of course, Alice. I will allow you anything.

Before the weekend is over, and Mr and Mrs Callao, and Linang, and Alice, return to Manila, Alice returns to me with a third line:

'How about this, Haruki?' She tells me:

Father, father

It is always Spring

Where you are.

'It has just the right amount of vagueness, don't you think Haruki? In your mind, and maybe say, in your heart, your father means eternal springtime. Please forgive me if I've overstepped. I will accept happily if I am wrong.' She searches my eyes.

I tell my eyes to keep a blank look, but I know from the way Alice relaxes her gaze that she knows she is right—that she has perfectly ended my poem. I am too dumbfounded to say anything.

'I'll see you next month, Haruki,' she only says. 'Goodbye, Ms Alice,' I only say. And then, I quickly remember myself. 'Thank you, Ms Alice.'

All at once she is my *kijo* and *kireji*, and whatever sublime marriage they can make of themselves in the last line. Alice reconciles all my aspects to my one self. Alice is my third line.

Part Two

1921-1935

Salvacion, 1922

It is my older brother, Francisco, who has been the acting *padre de familia* in our family—despite the fact that our parents are still alive. It is Francisco who wants to alter what seems like an already steady course as an average Filipino family—one that neither dreams too big nor too small, but simply is. I am more than happy to let things continue as they are. I am more than happy to be afforded all my creature comforts, which include, but are not limited to, short walks in the city accompanied by a maid who holds an umbrella over my head, whether it is to church, or to the bay; but Francisco insists I should not be so content.

He wants me to make something of myself, but I am sixteen years old. I take pleasure in the things that please me—I do not take pleasure in the future.

The days go slowly and uneventfully. Francisco wants to be the youngest chief justice, which makes him curt and short with us morning and night—we are marginal to him because we cannot actually help him realize his dreams.

Suffice it to say that he does not especially take kindly to us. Us meaning our ageing parents, Jorge and Dolores Corazon, me, and an almost useless, handsome brother, Felix. Felix and I understand each other in a way we will never understand Francisco. Beyond duty is love, and Francisco has not yet seen us beyond the bounds of duty. He does not love us.

I suppose he must be serious because he cannot be handsome. Felix, on the other hand, is handsome and is never serious. Felix will not dream big for his family, because he cannot even dream big for himself. Perhaps because we exist quite beyond his dreams, I can safely say that Felix loves us. Felix who lives every day according to its ways and appetites.

We knew early on that Felix needed to be set right. Studying to be a doctor was, our mother decided, the way to ease into high status. If he played his cards right, and married the right girl, he would well be on his way to the *tertulias* in all the oldest Manila homes. But young doctors know nothing about card games—sure they know how to play a hand, and sure, they pride themselves on knowing how to play at life; but in his twenties, Felix only knows how to play a good card game, he does not yet know how to play at life.

He, however, knows a heady game we all know—but whether he can play it, or it can play him, remains to be seen. I mean an ancient play let's, you and I, call desire, and how, when seen in just the right light and from just the right angle, it so closely resembles love.

Felix, though, is one step ahead of us in this game. He knows his appetites do not mean love, but they can mean a hunger as strong *as*; that given the right moment and the right girl, desire can make a man forget himself, and who he is, and where he's from— for the eleven minutes it takes to have a girl. He will love her for all those eleven minutes. He will turn from her on the twelfth.

Shortly after he graduated from medical school at the Universidad de Santo Tomás, Felix was sent on a medical mission in Bukidnon, a southern province long days by boat from Manila.

While there, he meets another hazel-eyed, fair-complexioned beauty named Segunda Sixto. She is his stationed nurse. Little is known of her, except that she is of mixed parentage, perhaps a dash Spanish and Chinese; rumour allows her father is German, come to the islands for a bit of wealth.

So the son of a middle class, aspirational family meets the beautiful mestiza of dubious provenance, and certainly not of the family's desired class.

Of course, Segunda catches his eye that first time he reaches for a scalpel, or the first time she tenders a stethoscope on what should just be a routine tapping of a local's lungs. Let's say it's late 1921. He is a little homesick and it's three months to Christmas. He is thinking of our mother's honey cake, the one festooned with yellow butter flowers on each corner. He is telling Segunda this while tapping into the lungs of a seven-year-old *barrio* boy. He is telling her she reminds him a little of our mother, in that she feels like home.

That night, a hazy tropical night punctuated by the churr of crickets and the biting threat of mosquitoes, he goes to her. And this is where the story actually begins. On a hospital cot in a nurse's dormitory called *Providence* in Bukidnon. It is ensconced in mosquito nets. He is homesick, and she reminds him of our mother, or, more specifically, our mother's buttered honey cake. She is thick like that, overwhelming like that. 'Honey,' he says, 'honey.' And, just like that, on a hot, tropical night, Alice Feria is conceived.

The next day, Felix cannot meet Segunda Sixto's searching eyes. When he asks for the stethoscope, it is with surgical coldness.

That is when she knows that whatever happy ending she imagined was within white grasp the night before, does not exist in the cold light of morning. Segunda Sixto asks for a transfer. She does not yet know that she is with child.

Felix Feria returns home soon after, our mother's full pride. Come Christmas, and tenderly indulged with our mother's famous honey cake, he is full of warm feelings. He allows himself to think of Segunda. *Where are you now*, he thinks, *where are you now.*

Where she is now is in Bukidnon, in her German father's house—she has just told her father and her mother that she is with child. Her father wants to strike her with his own father's walking cane. He is about to brandish, against her cowered figure, its curved, hard wood. He will kill him, he tells his daughter, *him* being Felix Feria, blissfully unaware in his buttered world. Who is he, and what is his name, he asks his cowering daughter. *Feria*, she says, *Felix.*

At this moment, Felix is eating his cake. It is a lush, moist sponge, 'heaven in a slice,' he tells his mother. *Mi hijo,* she says, *mi hijo.* My son. He does not tell her his true sentiments, the way two anti-heroes in a novel published at roughly the same time, tell a delicate girl their true sentiments—that a man needs a good girl to marry, and a bad girl to play around with. By 'good girl,' he means a girl approved of by his mother. By 'bad girl,' he means Segunda Sixto, who is not a bad girl, but she becomes one, a little later on in this story, in our mother's narrative.

In a scant ten months we receive a telegram in our Cabildo home that Felix has just sired a daughter with Segunda Sixto, and that he—should he be so inclined—might want to look at his child in San Lazaro Hospital in Manila, close enough to his home to manage a visit.

Felix denies his paternity to our mother but I know better. Playing the odds, I know that there is the slightest chance that the child in San Lazaro Hospital is Felix's child. On a hunch, I make my way to the hospital, bracing myself for what might come next.

What I see is the mother. What I see is the basket on which is ruggedly, carelessly laid the most beautiful baby I have ever seen. The baby's eyes are brown; her skin is white, as white as those *Americano*s I have seen along Escolta, Manila's commercial centre.

I had given Segunda Sixto five hundred pesos for a treasure. It was, to me, the biggest haggle of my life. I did not bring the basket to my older brother—I brought the handled, sad weave to our mother instead. Felix might be a doctor and he will know how to deal with sundry barrio ailments, but he will not know what to do with a surprise child. My mother sees the child and weeps, *mi hijo*. The baby's nose is not our nose, it is pinched and will be aristocratic—but you can already see, despite their lightness, that these are Felix's eyes.

As Wood to a Fire, 1921

Every day she cools his body down with a cloth doused in cold water. She will start mid-foot, squeezing water on each soft, white arch. She will then drown the cloth in the basin, squeeze out the excess water and move on to each of his armpits. In those hollows, his hair is light and spare as a boy's.

This she does repeatedly until the fever abates for short minutes. And then she will use a fresh towel to cool his head—dousing the cloth once then twice. She will rest the cloth on his wet forehead with a damp hand until she feels his body loosen into sleep.

Some nights there are chills before the fever. When they come, she rubs his back gingerly, and wraps the thin sheet snugly around his shivering body. When he sleeps, she watches his head turn right then left in violent snatches. When he cries out in his sleep, she wakes him, strokes his hair, says 'Doctor Feria, you are having a bad dream.' Sometimes he sleeps deeply at the sound of her voice; sometimes he wakes, starting, in the dark. His hold leaves marks as red as mangosteen rind on her wrists. When he is in his right mind, he says don't leave me, and she says no, no, in a voice so reassuring, his grip slackens and he falls asleep.

In the morning, there is a fever, a damp brow, an almost feral shine in his eyes. She lifts the tonic to his mouth, and he sips it from a shallow bowl with a grimace. 'Sixto,' he will say, 'Have you been watching me in my sleep again?' She had felt her face flush feverishly the first time he had asked this. Both times since, she has retorted, gamely, 'Yes doctor, I'm the only one in the city brave enough to see you so —' a beat, and then, 'unwell.' 'Is unwell a *eufemismo*?' he will ask with amusement. 'Is "*eufemismo*" code for *feo*?' she will answer. At this he will laugh his deep-throated laugh, then feel the nausea slip into him. 'Do you always answer a question with a question?' He will ask. 'What do you mean?' She will answer.

When the chills stop and it is only the fever left, she will ask another nurse to watch Doctor Feria so that she can attend to the other patients. When he spies other hands administering his tonic—other hands holding damp cloths to his feet, his armpits, his forehead, he brushes them away almost violently; he does not care that his wrists cast a hurting, backhanded flick.

When she returns, he looks at her almost superciliously. 'Where have you been?' He will ask. 'Did you think you were my only patient, Doctor Feria?' There you go again with the questions, he will say. His brows will cross at the same time an amused smile lifts the left corner of his mouth.

She will note that the fevers are fewer and far between, and that the cool air from the mountains has kept the sweat from his forehead—that his dry head reveals a thick bale of black hair. She has seen that hair wet, and stroked it back as a mother would. Now she sees the curl on his forehead, the redness slip back into the tips of his ears, his mouth. 'Oh,' she tells herself. And then, again, 'Oh.'

Felix, 1921

Between Francisco and my parents haranguing me to make something of my life, there is little space to breathe. Each time I find myself in a Manila tertulia, in one of those grand houses, in one of those mansions whose masters are named Roxas, or Ayala, or Guerrero, and I am asked my name, and I tell it to them in full, the one question I am asked is 'Feria. Are you Francisco's brother?'

The first time I was asked the question, I felt a deep pride, a kind of swell in the heart, a kind of squareness in the shoulder. It meant that my brother was making a name for himself even in Manila's highest circles with the elite, and with the elite's daughters. And then, as more and more tertulias happened, and I heard Francisco's name mentioned so often, the name began to hurt my ears. Francisco. A felicitous name, a saintly name. His would not be a life with snatches of casual magic. He would make that magic happen. And then I say my name. Felix. A name more whip than song.

In the one family picture that we have, my parents sit on chairs facing the photographer. Our sister Salvacion sits between them on a white chair. Francisco and I stand behind them. He tilts slightly so that his right arm rests on the back of Salvacion's chair, his left arm fastened to his side like a soldier at rest. I, too, rest an arm on our sister's chair but I suppose the tilt of my body seems more natural, my other arm like a dark sail when I hold my hand to my hip. I did not think I carried my body this way, but I have always felt at home in it. And when women look at me—eyes wide when they are just past childhood, slyly when they are older, lowering their eyes when they pass me in the street—I feel even more at home in it. I see in their eyes a confirmation of what I have always known: my body isn't so much a temple as an empire shaped by its own appetites. I do not need to say how I have acquired the narrowness of my hips or the sleekness of my torso.

A childhood strain on Francisco's lungs had kept his back hunched, his shoulders tense, his fear of losing and taking breath, both, giving his eyes a wary squint. Family lore has it that Francisco had stopped breathing once as a young child, and that mama had pledged to be a '*madre*' if Christ would be so merciful as to let her baby breathe again. Christ *was* merciful, and yet mama did not become a nun—she had become a mother twice more after Francisco.

I believe that that broken promise had its own consequences. Sometimes I believe that he sent me to her as her punishment and trouble. And her joy, I'm sure, though she will not admit it. I have seen her eyes shine after Francisco scolds me after one travesty or other. After one travesty or other, when she lets me kneel on salt to atone for my 'sins' before the altar, I see how she wipes away a tear before she is drawn either to the master's bedroom or to the kitchen, either by my father or our help, depending on who is with her when I cause her grief. Because this is a Christian household, the guilt far outweighs the sin.

As a child, my sins were falling asleep during rosary, or bringing tadpoles in from the rain, or leaving a frog under my yaya's pillow before she retired to bed. At first, I would be led—kicking and elbowing my way—to the altar on which stood Our Lady of Remedios with her ivory hands and ivory face and long lashes and her eyes looking at me beseechingly, never reprovingly like Francisco. I was never sorry for my sins but I was always very, very sorry I had made such an exquisite lady cry.

Her eyes grated on me much more than the salt ever did on my knees. The older I grew, and my sins increased in both magnitude and thrill—that one time lifting the skirt of the neighbour's girl Carmen, that other time stealing the ivory hands of San Bartolome from the parish church—for I would never go for San Sebastian, or San Juan, or San Pedro—and never ever for Sto Niño, you must understand that I am not entirely a heathen—I would lie leisurely on my bed until they came for me. They came for me in the morning for I often did my misdemeanors at night (the exception being Carmen whose skirt I had lifted one Sunday morning on the way home from Church). They came for me not with any warning or weapon. When I was ten years old, they came to me with Francisco who was worse than both, being five years my senior, and already an insufferable little man at the old age of fifteen. The older I got, they did not have to seize me at all from bed, for I would already be waiting for them at daybreak. They did not have to slap me awake, I was already awake, singing a little ditty under my breath, or whistling under my teeth. They came for me when I was ready for them—for I knew all the buttons I could push—and their religious airs, their fear of losing face and name among our old rich neighbours. I was the criminal ready for punishment. The older I grew and they edged into my room before the sun was even up, I would already be in my day clothes, leading them, as they led me to the altar, to their consternation and my giddy pleasure.

I do not remember Francisco ever having to kneel in front of the altar. I do not believe the bones of his knees have ever known as well as mine have the sharp grind of salt; I do not believe his form has ever brought my mother tears.

Salt before an altar is a forever punishment for a child because the minutes seem like hours, the crime larger than it actually is, the mother's disappointment always deeper than it should ever be. The practice is meant to cause so much pain in one's childhood that a child has no recourse but to change his ways to spare himself from future pain.

I am twenty-one and still I kneel before the altar. Sometimes with Salvacion who is more and more like me every day. A willing and staunch ally and a proud family shame. When my parents point to Francisco as a model Salvacion and I must pattern our lives after—and we see his slight build and his pinstriped suit and his thinning hair that so much resemble his righteousness and arrogance, we nod, keeping our laughter in check until they go from the room. And then when we know it is only Francisco who hears, Salvacion and I finally let go. Our heads roll with laughter as Francisco glares at us across the room where he has been asked to keep watch over us.

In the one family picture we have, the one I have told you about, the one that sits on the wooden table on the landing by the mirror festooned and framed with curlicues and dots, my father and my brother wear the same kind black bowtie, only my father wears a white suit and Francsico wears a pinstriped one. They are almost the same person at different stages of life. Francisco slips his hand between the buttons on the left side of his shirt like a young Napoleon. This picture perfectly captures all the difference between us. *The Prince and the Peacock*, Salvacion calls us—I do not think I need to explain which is which and who is who. When I see how different we are in this photograph, when I can tell that I am more pleasing to the eye, when I see how my coat falls on my shoulders, how the coat clutches my torso, then and only then do the scales seem to balance. Francisco can be the ambitious one if he wants, I will be the happy one.

In these tertulias, the ladies do not take to him. He does not wear his clothes well, he wears his clothes like my father with his scrappy dimensions and old man's shoulders.

His hair thins on his crown even as he is not yet thirty. When he converses with a lady and he talks about the insular American government—to a lady!— I have seen them cover their yawns with the backs of their hands before they excuse themselves. Such ladies meet my eyes from across the room where I watch my brother's comedic interactions. They smile at me; if they are pretty, I wink. If they are pretty, I brush the hair on my forehead. And then I saunter to them, swoop in. 'Amor, you will be the death of me,' I tell them. When their parents aren't watching, I let my forefinger brush their earlobes. If they are weak of constitution, they turn weak-kneed, and are helped to the stringy seats of mariposas by their sisters or maids or, to my embarrassment, their mothers.

If I am successful with the ladies, Francisco is successful with their parents. To them, I am a daughter's fancy and he is a prospect.

When Francisco and I go to houses where there are willing girls, I think of the good girls when I nestle my head between their navels and their moist places. There, I kiss. They are called Nenang and Maria, but when I reach my joy, I call them Dolores, I call them Trinidad, I call them Carmen, I call them any one of the names of the rich girls I've met in houses with foyers, where they carry the trains of their skirts up grand staircases and then throw them gracefully on the landing where the cloth cascades—their *trajes de mestizas* held together with diamond brooches; their hair fastened by *paynetas* festooned with round pearls and marquise diamonds.

The girls I cannot resist are the ones with cameos on velvet chokers around their necks. They want me one night, and they do not want me the next night, until I kiss their wrists behind dark stairwells or in gardens that smell like stars and *jasmin*. Because I will not go beyond their wrists or their earlobes, or their hair, I carry my appetites and my sex elsewhere. To simpler girls who wear rouge and cheap perfume, their hair down, and their moans easy.

And then I walk home to Cabildo Street.

On one such night, I had seen Francisco in the dark *sala*, the red end of his cigar sputtering devilishly, or as badly-intentioned.

When do you think you'll be done with this pastime of yours? I hear him say in the darkness.

When will you be done with yours? I ask him.

Don't you think I'm done planting?

Don't you think I'm too young to be done planting?

Must you always answer a question with a question? he asks.

If I answered a question with an answer, what else would be there to talk about? I tell him.

He turns the gaslight two notches to the right, and looks at me from head to toe. His disapproval makes me cocky. I answer his glare with a smile.

Sin verguenza, you are absolutely and utterly hopeless, he tells me.

Well, I don't know about that—I've had my fair share of luck tonight.

And with that, I unbutton my coat, and waltz with myself giddily until I reach my room. I hear Francisco walk with heavy feet to his quarters, hear him slam the door, his anger proportional to my happiness at having caused it.

The only time I see Francisco's approval are on the nights he and I stay home, and I have no recourse but to bury my head in my medical books. My father is too old to father me now—and Francisco sees this when the old man needs his baston more and more just to cross the distance from the living room to the master's bedroom. This takes ten of my father's shuffles and two of my long strides (there are few other ways a person can tell a man's strength and heartiness than by the way he walks, or shuffles, or strides). When the old man shuffles, I know that he does not have too much time left on this glad earth—that it worries him that he may not live long enough to see me right myself. It is one of the few things that cause me grief.

When I am home during such evenings, Francisco then draws on his cigar contentedly as I mention human anatomy from my books. Secretly, I study the caves of the places I have been to. Francisco asks me what parts of the body I am studying, and I say the skull: the secrets of my *sentido* common, or lack of it. Really, I am studying places I have been to: labia minora, and then labia majora, and I remember the round place, small as a peanut that I had clenched between my teeth not two days ago, but just last night when Francisco had gone to bed, thinking he had left me with my books.

But these days have started to feel like heavy days. These days I never seem to get any joy from any of my usual entertainments—from the coy stylings of the girl I am courting to the stirrings of the girl whose bed I share. They seem to me to be two versions of the same girl, and the days bleed into each other, and the girls I know bleed into each other until they seem like one long day and one long girl. These days the meals start late and the wine starts early. And every next glass of wine is a failure to relive the effervescence of the first one. And when I turn to my books, the words do not seem blurry at all, they seem to come with their own voice, announcing themselves: *hueso occipital, hueso temporal, mandibula.* And then it is suddenly Sunday again and already, and here we are in our pew and Francisco has just stamped my father's *baston* on my left foot to make me listen more attentively to the Gospel, or so I think, only he whispers in my ear the words of Christ himself: *se hace.* It is done. I don't know what he means until I do, until what he had spoken of two nights before had seeped back into my memory when he had told me about Nenang, and what trouble I was in, and had said he would take care of it.

A Clearing Ready for Burning

They clear the forests here to grow *mais* and sweet potatoes and once the harvest is over, they clear the land again, this time by burning it. They call this the fallow year—the year the weeds and roots are burned so that new crops can be grown.

In fields, Felix sees sugarcane—cut down with cane knives with long wooden handles and flat, wide blades with curved hooks on their cutting side. The blade is thin but when the wielder slashes at an angle, the cut is clean and quick. He cannot hear the sound but he can see the rhythm in the cutter's movements.

They call the people here mountain dwellers—though the real mountain dwellers have travelled deeper into the hinterlands. When Felix arrives, he sees mountains beyond the sugarcane fields, their stalks thin, their leaves spry and green. And then he sees pockets of burning.

The terrain rolls until it reaches a small town, the houses made of palm leaves and bamboo walls. He has seen versions of these houses with stilts under them, but these houses are fenced off with a latticework of bamboo stalks. Unlike the ones he's seen, the lower area is fenced off.

It was the Americans who called these *nipa* huts, field houses in rural areas, but even his house on Cabildo Street in Manila is structured the same way, only with sturdier and more expensive materials—a stone base instead of bamboo, a tiled roof instead of palm leaves. But here is the same elevated floor, the same high roofs and wide windows. The windows here are kept open by a wooden rod holding the top of the window to the sill. In Felix's home, the windows are decorated with squares of mother of pearl, and slide open into a wide Manila Street.

He imagines that this must look like the place where his parents grew up before they had been brought by Francisco to Manila from Iloilo, but this place is lusher, its terrain more rolling. It is a place of sunshine, laced, he thinks to himself, with a danger he can't explain. The light is heavy, feels chased or menaced by a steady darkness.

The journey here had been the longest journey of his life— one week to Iloilo and then another two days to here. Those were long days and short nights, for the nights were equipped with boys-turned-doctors and there were always card games and whisky on the deck. The days were long even if one woke after noon. In glaring daylight, the ocean which had seemed at first to Felix like a beautiful distance between him and Manila, an infinite dazzle of sun on water, and high wind, now seemed like an infinite loneliness.

He had not told his family that he had been sent on a medical mission here, had not even left a note for his father or Francisco. He had only stolen into Salvacion's room before daybreak, and tickled her cheek to wake her. She had looked at him suspiciously from head to toe, had seen him in his second-best Americano, had known he was saying goodbye.

She pressed her lips together to keep from crying. He had put his finger to his lips and had told her that he would be away for a while but that he would write her a letter every month, and then another one for their mother. He had told her that she was to break the news to their mother gently—*gently, Salvacion, no theatrics*, he had said, and *not until after lunch.*

Where are you going? She had asked, and he had said *somewhere far,* but that he would return, she could count on it. *You owe me twenty-five centavos every day you're away,* she had told him, and he had said, *I might make you a rich lady yet,* and she had said *rich enough to marry me off to an Ayala? No,* he had said, *but maybe rich enough to marry you to new rich like Francisco. You won't be gone very long then* she had said, and then they had both laughed, and then he was gone. Looking out into the ocean, he realized that this was the only conversation he'd had in months that brought him real joy.

The sea had started to feel like a long loneliness during daytime, and an ache at night—thank God for the boys who sang when the boys who lost at card games grew violent and threatened to throw each other overboard—these were also the same boys who could easily be diverted with a love song or with a *kompañero's* warm arm around his shoulder. And then there were the Rizalistas who recited the national hero's *Mi Ultimo Adios* where it was meant to be recited—in a boat full of idealistic young men, their fates uncertain, the stars never as clear as when they'd shone over them.

It was only under stars that Felix had completely comprehended Rizal's words—only the hero had written the words hours before his death, and had stashed the poem in a lamp and had bequeathed the lamp to a woman he had married mere hours before his death in Fort Santiago, kilometres from Cabildo Street where Felix had spent his formative years.

Everyone knew that Rizal's greatest love was his country. How must that have felt, Felix had thought, to the woman that he married:

> *Adios, Patria adorada, region del sol querida,*
> (Goodbye land that I love, land loved by the sun,)
> *Perla del Mar de Oriente, nuestro perdido Eden!*
> (Pearl of the orient sea, an Eden we've lost)
> *A darte voy alegre la triste mustia vida,*
> (Gladly do I give you this hopeless life)
> *Y fuera más brillante más fresca, más florida,*
> (Had this life been more brilliant, had this life more newness, more youth)
> *Tambien por tí la diera, la diera por tu bien.*
> (I would give it to you still; I would give it still for your good)
> ...
> *Ensueño de mi vida, mi ardiente vivo anhelo.*
> (My enchantment, my ardent love)
> *Salud te grita el alma que pronto va á partir!*
> (I toast to your health as my soul takes flight)
> *Salud! ah que es hermoso caer por darte vuelo,*
> (I toast to your health! O how good it is to die for you to rise!)
> *Morir por darte vida, morir bajo tu cielo,*
> (To die so that you live! To die under your sky!)
> *Y en tu encantada tierra la eternidad dormir.*
> (Under your magical ground, to sleep for eternity)

Felix does not think that this respite in Bukidnon will be his final farewell but the words move him just the same. He is not in middle age, the way Rizal was in middle age, dying at thirty-five. And what Rizal fought for not thirty years ago was freedom from Spain, a colonial master to the Philippines for more than three hundred years. Felix, at twenty-five, does not know exactly if he must die for anything at all. The year is 1921, and Rizal has been dead for twenty five years. He cannot be sure that Rizal would know exactly what the hero was dying for—for after the great revolution of 1896, Spain had sold the Philippines to America in 1898, and Spain had ceded the Philippines, Guam and Puerto Rico to America for twenty million dollars. Felix asks himself if Rizal would have risked his life knowing what would eventually happen to the country he was born in, and had died for, but this question burns him for only a scant minute.

And then he remembers his ultimate goodbye to Manila—which had only ever been to parents he loved, a brother he hated, a sister he had doted on, a good girl he had only halfheartedly courted, and a bad girl he might have truly loved.

His ultimate goodbye was an ultimate goodbye to all the tertulias in all the houses of the old rich, and the rich dinners in the houses of the new rich, and the confusion of his older brother as to where exactly his own family had belonged in the greater scheme of things. He would not now think of Nenang and the love she had offered him in those dark hours in that dark street before he walked home to Cabildo—to Francisco's blunt disapproval, to the embers of the righteous cigars of a man who cared so much for the place his family kept in polite Manila society that he was prepared to sacrifice his own happiness, and the happiness of his only brother.

This was not a hero's goodbye, this was the typical goodbye of a typical Filipino man of his time—more specifically, this was the typical goodbye of a second son who did not have to carry his parents' expectations of a first son, but who would be made aware of his position in life by a first son. He could not marry a girl he loved, he would be asked to marry a proper girl he may or may not love—one who would elevate his family steadily into the follies and starts of an affluent Manila family.

The reality had so ired him on this boat that he had been every kind of boy—he had been the rowdy boy threatening to throw the boy with a winning card hand overboard; and he had been the singing boy who had assuaged at least one violent boy from his murderous inclinations. He had also been the Rizalista who had recited all fourteen stanzas of what many Filipinos had proclaimed to be the very best poem by a Filipino. He was all kinds of boys because he was the most troubled boy in the high seas between Manila and Iloilo. If he had disappeared now, his death would not have been an important death in the least—and there were worse deaths to disappear to than an ocean speckled by stars and lit with the songs of young boys who did not know where they were going, but who were certain that it was the best place to serve as young men and as young doctors.

The name Bukidnon had seemed as exotic to him as the names Paris or Madrid or London. It was a place so far away from Manila that it might as well have been found on a separate continent. He did not know if he was excited or scared to be travelling to such a place.

And then he had arrived to a place where he knew no one and no one knew him, save the rowdy gaggle of boys he had arrived with. The knowledge had brought him a lightness of heart that he hadn't felt in years. When his sight had travelled from field to mountain and then from mountain to new field, the view had felt like a new life, something so wide and so far that he had begun to feel infinite. The miracle of it all to Felix was that such a feeling could exist, and that feeling was an entire world, and it had held Felix so readily and so completely in its grip that if anyone had asked him what his name was at that precise moment, he wouldn't have known what to tell them.

And so Felix had arrived in that harbour, not wholly afraid, but not wholly certain of what lay before him. He had been pushed by necessity into that first boat, and then by force into a second one en route to a destination neither his parents nor Francisco had ever spoken about, apart from the fact that it was a long boat ride from Iloilo.

What lay beyond Iloilo was anybody's guess. Talk from the boat had it that the people in this place were mostly indigenous but partly Christianized and Felix did not know exactly what that meant, only that it bred in him a kind of comfort and a kind of fear, possibly less the former and more the latter.

When he had ridden into town with only a fellow doctor and a guide on a single horse, he had seen the most breathtaking view he had ever seen; it had seemed to him more ancient and primordial than Manila, among whose stones and fortifications he had grown up. The hills rolled here as they had only done in picture books about America in the 1800s. It had only ever seemed to him like cowboys and Indians in that picture book, but in this reality, he did not know if he was the cowboy or the Indian.

He had seen, in wide stretches of field, more than two pockets of fire, and the local doctor had told him that indigenous people had burned a plot of land where they had previously grown sweet potatoes, and likely mais, and that both had been harvested, and that now the land was being cleared of both the weeds and the roots of the harvest to make way for a new harvest next year. 'But next year is ten months away,' Felix had told him, and the doctor had said that the year Doctor Feria and his fellow doctors had arrived would be a fallow year, a rest year after the harvest—during the burning of both the old roots and the old weeds. This fallow year would be needed first, especially by indigenous farmers, the local doctor had said.

But Felix Feria had only heard the word *fallow*, and the word *harvest*, and had taken this year to mean the year he would sow small seeds for a harvest next year. He still hasn't grasped completely what this means to his presence here and now—he is a visceral, not an intellectual.

He only knows that it will mean something, maybe not right here or right now, but sometime in the near future. It will mean something.

Felix, 1921

The first time he had done a routine tapping of a local boy's lungs, the boy had worn clothes so strange to Felix that he had had to look twice at the boy before he remembered himself and realized that this was not Manila.

The boy had worn what looked like a red kerchief on his head, lined at the forehead with yellow piping. Small frisky balls attached to the lining fell from his forehead. Like his kerchief, his clothes were also red—the top matched his red pants. *A different kind of terno*, Felix thinks to himself. He remembers his mother and Salvacion's matching baro and saya—the top with short, butterfly sleeves, and its matching skirt.

The boy's red top is divided into precise squares, two on the boy's upper torso, and two where the cloth meets his waist. Embroidered within each square are small squares shaped like diamonds, forming now, in Felix' mind, a long vertical cross. The boy's shirt is buttonless and keeps to either side of his torso. He hides the space between the sides of his shirt with a thick beaded necklace, yellow like the lining of his head kerchief.

The beadwork matches the small diamond squares on his shirt. The necklace itself is so long that it falls to his navel.

Felix only sees a small sliver of torso—dark as Nenang's, three shades darker than his own skin. Given the boy's clothes, Felix knows that the boy might not be a Christian boy, and Felix has never met anyone not Christian. He does not quite know how to approach the boy.

Had this been Manila, he would have mussed his hair, or had offered a sweet, or had soothed him the way he had soothed Salvacion in her younger years. *Palangga*, he would have said but this boy is not a familiar. It is the first time in his life that he does not know how to conduct himself. Since he was a boy, Felix could charm anyone with his smiling eyes and curly hair. It becomes apparent that he cannot hold such court with this boy who looks at him warily, suspiciously. It is the only time Felix has not been able to win over a stranger.

The boy's heartbeat is faint against the stethoscope. It reflects almost faithfully the boy's demeanor. He seems to lack any kind of willful energy, and his face is pale compared to his hands and his torso. Felix feels the boy's forehead with the back of his hand, and then feels the boy's neck. He is burning with fever.

He would not know how to tell this to the boy's parents who are in the waiting room. He would not know how to interrogate them about the provenance of this fever, which is causing the boy so much discomfort, he looks to be seconds away from fainting.

He leads the boy to the waiting room gently, and tries explaining the predicament using tourist's sign. He holds the back of his right hand to his neck, and then the back of his right hand to his forehead and mimics a fainting spell. The boy's parents look at him quizzically and then look at each other in the same perplexed manner. They do not know if it is the boy who needs help, or if it is Dr Feria. He notes that there by their feet is their mode of payment—a basket of sweet potatoes and corn.

However this situation turns out, Felix thinks, he will never be hungry.

It is at that moment that he notices a fifth person in the room—he had forgotten that for every three doctors, there would be one nurse. She clears her throat from the corner of the hut where she has situated herself. 'Can I help you, Doctor Feria?' she asks in Spanish. 'The boy is burning with fever,' he tells her, 'and I will need to keep him here overnight. Do you speak the language? Can you explain this to his mother and father?'

'I believe so, Dr Feria,' she says. As she strides across the room, carrying her gas lamp, he sees her face. Her eyes are hazel like Our Lady of Remedios, and her hair falls in light brown curls on her forehead.

The nurse explains to the boy's parents in a dialect similar, though not identical to the one Felix's parents speak, that the Doctor wants to keep the boy overnight in his clinic. The parents look at each other and shake their heads at the nurse. 'It seems they want to bring him home tonight,' the nurse tells Doctor Feria. 'I can't in good conscience allow it, nurse,' Felix says. 'Can you please explain this to them?'

The nurse relays to the parents exactly what the doctor has asked her to.

The boys' parents shake their heads again, and lead the boy with them as they exit the hut. They carry with them the basket of food intended for Felix. 'Nurse,' Felix says, watching them go, 'I do not know what remedy they have for this boy's fever, but kindly explain that we have quinine and penicillin. Anything the boy may need.'

Again, the nurse explains what the doctor has told her to—but the mother and father only shake their heads. The father hitches up his son and carries him, and walks ahead of his wife down the wooden steps of the hut that is Doctor Feria's clinic (but that is also his home).

When the man and wife and their sick son leave, Felix turns to the nurse. 'Why couldn't you get them to stay?' he asks her. 'That boy is very, very sick.'

The nurse looks at him willfully, says, 'You are new to these parts, Doctor. These are parents who do not want to entrust their child to a stranger.'

'Surely, you're no stranger,' he tells her.

'No, but you are,' she says.

He sees the worry in her eyes but does not soften his voice. 'And what is to happen to that boy?' he asks her.

'They will decide what to do,' the nurse tells him. 'They will decide. Not you,' she says as she goes the way the boy's father went, down the wooden steps of the hut, into the new evening.

* * *

The next day, Felix asks Dominguez, his former classmate and neighbour, situated two huts from his, if he has met his nurse. Dominguez asks him his nurse's name. 'I wasn't able to ask,' Felix says, 'but maybe we share the same.' Dominguez asks Felix to describe her—'Light brown eyes,' Felix says, 'light brown hair that falls in a curly mop on her forehead.'

Dominguez tells him that they definitely do not share the same nurse, for his nurse is short and squat, and has black hair, the same colour as her eyes. Her physique is such, Dominguez elaborates, 'it is as though you had gotten a voluptuous woman and suddenly compressed her.'

'What is the name of your nurse?' Felix asks.

'Petra.'

'Petra?'

'I didn't think to ask for a last name,' Dominguez laughs.

Whatever the name of his nurse is, Feria decides for whatever his reasons, that it cannot be Petra.

Segunda Sixto, 1921

Segunda Sixto knows that the boy is very, very sick, and that if not attended to shortly, that he may die.

Unlike the doctors who have just arrived from Manila, she has lived here all her life. Her father is a German photographer, and her mother is a Cebuana—a native of Cebu. Far enough to be considered a journey but near enough so that they speak the dialect in the more urbanized towns in Bukidnon. Her father had come here to photograph the Manobo tribe, but he had seen her mother in the marketplace. A woman in traditional dress such as you may find in Cebu or Manila—without bothersome flourishes like tortoiseshell combs in her hair or pearls pressed into her ears. Segunda's mother had come to visit kin who had immigrated to these parts. She did not care to prolong the length of her visit. Segunda's father, on the other hand, had chosen to stay.

Segunda has seen her father's photographs. She knows they have not been featured in prominent international magazines. She sees photographs of Manobo men and women in their headdresses and their matching tops and trousers and skirts.

These seem to her like documentary photographs. She has seen them along with his photos of several trails and rivers leading to mountains beyond. Sometimes the trails can be seen up close, the photographer situated so closely to the foot of the mountain and on the trail itself that one cannot see how it winds. This is where she is right now, she thinks, she cannot see beyond the trail being situated so squarely on it.

Other times the trails are white serpentine slivers between two looming mountains. These are the only photographs of her father's that Segunda Sixto loves.

Her father's panoramic and natural views, however, are never published in *The National Geographic*, although it has long been his dream to find his photographs within its pages. The word in their home is that her father has never been published at all in any international magazine and that his photographs are only a kind of testimony to life in these parts and in this century—something he says he will pass on to his children as his legacy. As a child, Segunda had believed the story, but had found out that this was not quite true. Her father had been to her many things—hero, and teacher and first love—and, as it would happen, her first wound.

The first time Segunda Sixto had learned to distrust a man was when she had discovered in her parent's *baul* a particular issue of an international glossy. There below the photo of a bare-breasted and dark-skinned woman, not from these mountains but from mountains up North, was her father's byline. The woman had short hair that appeared unevenly cut— multiple kerchiefs were wrapped around her neck. Segunda had thought at first that this was the picture of a tribal man until her eyes moved downward and she had seen the woman's breasts.

The woman had been naked from her torso to her waist. She wore drawstring pants with an embroidery Segunda has not seen in these parts. The woman in the photo also wore bracelets that began on her left wrist and ended just before her left elbow. An entire row of copper covering the length of her entire arm.

Segunda had seemed indifferent to the photo until she had seen her father's name: Ferdinand Sixto, 1913 below the photograph. It seemed that her father had been published in an international magazine after all when she was fourteen years old.

She had never asked her father about this photograph, had never even mentioned seeing it. But she had understood then that her father had his secrets. The knowledge had been too much for her to bear at fourteen, but it isn't too much now at twenty-one.

All men, Segunda knows now, have their secrets, and to know the secret is to hate the man, which seems like a useless bit of wisdom to Segunda who is at that age where every man she loves is an adventure. She has not yet met the man who is her folly.

Salvacion, 1932

The day after Alice learns the truth about her mother, I decide it is time I bring her, now that she is ten, to Escolta. She will not wear any more of those sailor dresses—with its abominable short cape, and its atrocious hemline. It is time to buy her a proper young woman's clothes, even if they are a young American girl's clothes.

It is time to buy her a pair of gloves, and a flared skirt, and a collared top. It is also time to give her a significant piece of jewelry—perhaps pearl earrings; plain studs with a small *brilliantito* affixed to its end—nothing too elaborate or excessive, something that's just so. The old rich must know we aren't trying too hard, and the new rich must know that we can afford diamonds. It must be tasteful, but also telling.

Now that Alice has learned the source of her first hard wounds, it will be hard to shake her out of this particular stupor—but one must try. Alice who weeps at the slightest thing. Just this morning it had been a piece of music, yesterday it had been Danang the cook's paltry wages.

Had she been an ugly child, her tears would be unbearable. Good thing she is what every American stranger has called exquisite. I have thoughts about this but they are not pertinent now.

I saw an old starved dog outside yesterday, bones jutting out of its rib—an ugly dog, more scab than skin, and then not even of the pedigree good enough for the adoption of the old rich. Even then, it had seemed infinitely happier than Alice to be alive.

When Felix sent a telegram—to say that he had wired two hundred pesos to my account for a birthday gift for Alice—he was overcompensating the way he does every year.

He does this twice: once on her birthday, and once on Christmas. I want to tell him that she already knows the contents of every box delivered to her in his name. She has hidden her disappointment at what's inside—a doll, a teddy, a sailor's dress—for two years now. In his mind, she is always eight years old, although she is ten, not yet thick in the hips, but vast in her appetite.

I had sent him a telegram telling him as much. I admit that it was not a gentle telegram. I admit, further, that it was not a telegram and that it was a two-page letter. I admit, further, that it was more than two pages.

I had dark words for him, and dark words are not for telegrams, or two-page letters. I had told him to stop being a holiday father, seeing as the child has no real mother and needs a more consistent father figure in her life.

He had sent back a second telegram—and in it I sensed the sameness of our blood. That terseness and red leap. It takes a while for things to settle in Felix's mind. He is temperate first, and then impetuous after. I am impetuous first, and almost temperate after. But our impetuousness is volcanic. Thank God our tempers do not happen at quite the same time.

He had said—in that second telegram—and the gall of him to say it—that even if I am not the child's biological mother, I am her acting mother; and that unlike other motherless children who have had the great luck to be absorbed into proper Christian households, this particular child actually had my blood running through her veins.

It was a long telegram.

Of all the telegrams we have exchanged over the years, it was this particular telegram that Alice had to see. She had come home from school while I collected payment from my jewelry business. I had found her in the mail table in the foyer. Sat on a chair, tears in her eyes, telegram in her hands.

'What does this mean, mama?' she had asked me. 'What does what mean, Alicia?' I had asked more curtly than I had wanted. But I had sensed the situation was an emergency, and one can never be gentle in emergencies.

I had noticed her right hand trembling when she passed me the telegram.

My first thought when I had read its contents was that Felix was *such* a man. He was such a man. Only a man wouldn't have had the foresight to write a letter, as I had. What was writing a letter and stuffing it into a white envelope—what trouble was that—

I didn't bother telling her to ask her father what his meaning was—which is what so many of my contemporary women would have told their children when their children have discovered a parent's indelicacies.

Her father is hundreds of miles away, resting comfortably in his hacienda; his life like my father's life: leisurely and slow and curated by all the women in the household. He cannot even be troubled to write a letter, or to think that a child could very conceivably chance on the open contents of a telegram.

It is almost as if he cannot think, and that he needs a woman to think for him.

(To be fair, such a woman in his household would not have known how to deal with the contents of his telegram. But also, to be fair, he should not have been the kind of man who could so grieve a wife with the contents of his telegram).

He is man enough to think that there are things his wife is too delicate to bear, but he is not man enough to think there are things that his daughter, all of ten, is too delicate to bear.

And so, I have to explain to my delicate niece what her father cannot. I tell her that her mother was a princess in a distant island called Bukidnon. I tell her that her mother was of too high a pedigree—too royal a bloodline—to marry someone so common as her father. I tell her that her mother and father conceived her in love, but that her mother's father, a proper sultan, had not agreed to the match. 'But I thought that my father was a rich man,' she had said. 'Rich does not mean royal, Alicia,' I had countered.

And so I had said that her father had returned, quite broken-hearted to his mother in Manila (that is not an untruth), and that nine months later, an emissary from the sultan himself had delivered her to her father's home on Cabildo Street.

She had understood this story. 'Then theirs was a love forbidden,' she says to me at last. I sigh outwardly, but clench my fists. 'Yes, Alicia, then theirs was a love forbidden.' 'Oh how sad, she says, how very, very sad, mama. So—what you're telling me is that I'm half princess and half commoner?'. 'Yes, Alice—half princess and half commoner in blood.' She seems heartened and heartbroken all at the same time.

I am happy I have eased the child for now. Which does not mean that at this very moment—this quite provocative, quite cruel moment—I do not want to kill Felix.

Salvacion, 1935

Felix is largely absent from his daughter's life, but is grandly and excessively present in her milestones. Hearing that she loved Chopin, he had given her a practice piano on her thirteenth birthday. Hearing that her friend Linang had all the chicest Parisian fashions, he had sent me five hundred pesos to buy her the same European clothes. I had sent, instead, Alicia to Escolta, to buy the more affordable replicas.

With the excess, I had bought an art deco brooch I will give to Alice on her wedding day. In Escolta, I bought her two expensive dresses to receive her father on those two days of the year when he visits: Alice's birthday, and New Year's Eve. He has never spent a single Christmas with us, and never a New Year's Day. But to see Alice would be to believe that she has the richest father in the world.

Given her looks and bearing, locals immediately assume she is from the old families in Ermita.

Salesgirls brandish only replicas of the finest French fashions as soon as we entered fashion establishments. Such efforts they would not have extended to me. I have no illusions about my bearing. It is a point of pride for me to have adopted such an exquisite child and to have these so-called modern women fawn all over Alice—whose lightness of eye and skin and hair haunt them when they look at themselves in the mirror.

I had brought up Alice when I was little more than a child myself. At a time when my good-for-something brother Francisco, already a lawyer, and already an important man despite being just a few years older than our brother Felix, had set us up on Cabildo Street and had spread the story that I was a sister, widowed by a white scientist in Bukidnon, who had died from bad water; that I was here for a change of scenery—so much had 'widowhood' changed me that I was no longer my old, dulcet and loving self.

He had told his fellow *cabaristas* that he only wanted to restore me to my old humour. He told them this so that they would tell their wives. With that fable he had spun, he knew that pity would have coloured their first valuation of me and Alice. That pity, Franciso knew, would lead to acceptance.

I had raised the child with little more than five hundred pesos and all my mother's good jewelry. I had sapphire earrings, and a brilliant five-carat diamond—a wedding gift from my father to Felix, when he had seen that my brother had finally made a good match in Dolores: a 'proper Christian lady,' and not a loose woman from Bukidnon.

Francisco's white scientist story, I know was spun in honour of the woman's father—a white German photographer who had found a new Galapagos in Bukidnon—Francisco's words, not mine—with an exotic native who gave him Segunda Sixto, a strange, elusive, hybrid animal; a freak of nature.

When the money had run out—Alice was only two years old—I had decided to sell my parents' wedding gift. That diamond tided us over for a few more years with Francisco's help. I had sold the diamond to a Chinese jeweler in Manila who had given me two thousand pesos for it, as well as a diamond brooch. That brooch I sold to Francisco's friend who had had an indiscretion and was presently making up for it to his wife with an expensive bit of jewelry.

When I noticed these negotiations between husbands and wives, I knew I never wanted to be married. Why marry when all the men in my life—my brother not least—want only relations with bad women, and to end the day with their good wives? Even making love seems like a sham phrase. When Felix had told me, at sixteen, that he lived for that shuddering relief, it had only seemed to me that all men want is to relieve themselves inside their women, good or bad, and that it must be quite like a taking a piss, and I most definitely did not want to be pissed in.

Part Three

Manila: 1940-1941

Zipper, 1940

In the prime of my life, I did not expect to be here, halfway across the globe in a town called Manila, twice-colonized and on the brink of war. Looks of it, it is not too far from America, given that Manila looks like any prosperous American town—it is every bit what I imagine an American town would be. To my mind, it is a new Washington with its neoclassical buildings. It is also a little bit of New York with its Art Deco edifices and fixtures. You see this in their movie theatres where the very posh watch the Manila Symphony Orchestra and their various plays.

My friend Lehman's wife who has been here for the past three years tells me that the Filipino rich in the old days visited the old continent to learn their politics and their literature. They came home and started revolutions against the Spanish with what they had learned overseas. What takes learning is that most of these revolutionaries did not even want revolutions, they wanted reform—that they dreamed of a nation where reform was not a holy designation but a normal state of affairs. When I look around the old town, I see quite another revolution—it is no doubt a cultural one with the heirs apparent of the rich revolutionaries using their education to bring back the latest architectural styles. Hence columns and ziggurats and theaters and *theatres*.

I would not be here if it weren't for my friend Lehman dying suddenly of a heart attack in the middle of Eroica—a piece he had been conducting for the Manila Symphony Orchestra here in the Philippines. I say selflessly because Lehman had no business travelling here when half his family were in Dachau. He had perhaps thought it best to save his life on American territory with his wife Agnes, and his son Zeke. I take it he couldn't pay his way to a passport to America, and so he had thought to find himself the next best thing. A colony of.

It was mostly Lehman's forethought and survivor's instinct that made me admire him. He knew early on that he was not a composer, he was a conductor. He also knew early on that I was a composer and not a conductor, that I saw the moving parts, but not the whole.

The difference between us, perhaps, being that he had found himself in Manila when I had found myself in Dachau. He had escaped the camp I found myself in and plotted to find his way to America. He did, in a sense, find America here.

Lehman thought I was a good composer, but that I was not naturally a survivor. Once when I had come to him with some small brokenness—I don't know if it was a girl or a row with my father, he had put his arm around me and said, 'Herbert, you will do great things but you must learn first how to be a survivor. You must have a public self and a private self, and you must allow the world to meet your public self, but you must never introduce it to your private self.'

Not even the best minds have it in them to know how to survive—sure, they can know when to play a performative or abstract nocturne; they can read a room and know how to play it. But believe me, all those best minds have not always known how to slink away from an SS officer, and have not always known to bribe, with love or token, a gentile neighbour who would have spelled all the difference between life and Dachau.

I had expected to live out my war days in the old continent, perhaps gaining back some of the heart the concentration camps had stripped from me. I knew that I would not die in Dachau, but that I might die very shortly after in a place close to it.

Even in that desolate place, I did not lose my humour—that was part of the survival instinct I had trained in myself after what I had called the Lehman challenge. Humour came to me the minute I saw that German sign on the gates: work makes us free. This is an obvious transliteration, and must not come across cleanly to an ear accustomed to English. Translated, it must come closer to: work sets us free. *Arbeit Macht Frei.*

Which is an irony because we did not come to Dachau to work, we came to Dachau to die. Still, I had been inspired by those words to write a resistance song disguised as a workman's song. I did not have much to work with, some string, a matchbox, and the kindness of a German soldier who supplied both only a few short hours after I asked for them.

These were the only strings I had to work with. I had no musicians, but I had ten hungry men, likely sick with tuberculosis and dysentery, to gather into a makeshift orchestra. But there, in an outhouse in Dachau, we created a song hundreds could sing, hundreds who were dying every day. I would like to think that they marched to their deaths with their hearts and spirits high because they were singing a resistance song against the very Germans sending them to their deaths. I'd like to think they were fighting to the very end. Not just for their lives, but for a larger concept of humanity, of which they were an aching, important part.

Shortly after, I was transferred to Buchenwald. If Dachau was desolate, this place was a wasteland. In Buchenwald, there were no makeshift orchestras. In Buchenwald there were no outhouses in which to write and sing resistance ditties. When they transferred me to Buchenwald, I thought my life would end there.

What immediately struck me was that there were no birds in Buchenwald where there were birds in Dachau. When I awoke in Dachau, there was at least one fugitive bird that had given hope to my morning, a winged reminder that perhaps there was such a place as a thereafter apart from this concentration camp that did not mean death or heaven.

I learned shortly thereafter that escapees were hung from trees in the concentration camp. These bodies, hung still in their stripes, gaunt and sick, had likely scared away the birds. There were no birds in Buchenwald—if you didn't catch my drift the first time, perhaps you will catch my drift now and here.

For the first time in my life, I had begun to feel that kind of slow desolation that rises, little by little, slowly, slowly every day, that one hardly knows it is there. Until that one day when all those small deaths accrue into a kind of leaden weight one feels in the legs and in the arms. One cannot move from all that pain that manifests itself as an all-encompassing lack of feeling. That is how strong the pain really is. It cannot admit its own hurt to itself. For once, I would have gladly died in that bed smelling of shit, my hair shaved, my heart no longer a muscle but a kind of extraneous organ not part of myself but beating in spite of myself. It was then that I knew that spite was not a thing to take against a captor, but that spite was a thing to hold against one's self. For I did not want to be alive. Life, and my daily affirmation of it, was not something I wanted, as time went by.

One begins to understand then the heart is a deliberate but kind muscle. It does not tell the mind all that it holds;

until all that it holds, has felt, and has been feeling, becomes too unbearable. As a recourse it tells its secrets to the mind. The mind, tell-all beast that it is, reminds the body.

I had not wanted to move from my shit-and-lice laden bunk when the news had come in. My papa had written to the authorities for my release. This is one of the few kindnesses I have afforded my captors: they had approved it. Men like me who had served time in concentration camps could actually be petitioned for, as my father had petitioned for me. Old Jewish men who had not served as verifiable threats to the regime could, in their affable and small towns, and in their big cities too, make small appeals for their sons. Once in a blue moon, and by sheer luck, these appeals could be heard by men whose mothers had somehow raised them right.

As everything lucky in my life, everything thereafter was sudden. Suddenly, it was 1939, and suddenly, I was a 'free' man.

I have long held it that there are two sides to every man. Every man is part angel and part devil. For what was that day if not biblical that my father had appealed to a mere administrative clerk, and that clerk had listened to his better angel.

I had expected myself to die, lice and shit laden in Buchenwald not twenty-four hours before, when suddenly: I was free—the irony being that I had seen things that would haunt me all my life and behold me to them forever.

I had found my way to my homeland Vienna shortly thereafter. I had spent a week in papa and mama's arms—in the rest afforded to me by my childhood bed, in the comfort afforded to me by the chicken soup my mother had ladled night after night into my exhausted tongue. I had just that day made my way into my childhood garden when I received the news.

Lehman was dead.

Zipper, 1940

Agnes has set me up in an apartment in the old rich district of Ermita. She has made sure that there I have the bare essentials. It is what Lehman would have wanted, she tells me. Perhaps I am part of her denial that he is dead. That, through me, he has merely assumed a new form. I can't say I fully blame her. Who hasn't believed, in some way, that our gone loves aren't really gone, they simply assume a new form.

She is grieving Lehman the same way I am grieving my lost Dachau orchestra, or the family I may or may not see again in this life.

Perhaps it is my orchestra, acting through Agnes, who has ensured that by the time my boat arrives in Manila Bay, I already have a welcoming committee. Who isn't to say that it isn't my orchestra, acting through Agnes, who has ensured that I already have a small flat waiting for me, and that I have a Frigidaire filled with provisions—milk, eggs, and bread, and water. Who isn't to say that it isn't my orchestra, acting through Agnes, that makes her bury her head on my chest almost the second I greet her from the plank in Manila Bay? I have only seen Agnes once in my life but she touches me like I am an old familiar.

Agnes wants me to take three days to myself—to read the room, she says, when the room is really a city. Therefore I must really read a city, as far and near from my experience as death.

When she deposits me in my new flat, she gives me a phone number and an address where they have been billeted since Lehman brought her here. Dakota apartments, I note with a chuckle—a native American tribe appropriated by Americans to name a residential apartment in an American colony. How very appropriate, I think drily.

Agnes tells me to give her a call any old time I am lonesome, she says. She doesn't know that I am lonesome all the time, and that it is not an altogether bad thing. A part of me has been lonesome all my life—in all the good and bad ways—ever since I discovered Beethoven at fourteen; that first time my fingers had *glissandoed* into notes that had been written centuries before I was born. I had been born to play him, and he had only been born to create music as affecting as pop songs. I have played many a private concert in many a rich man's house, and I have only ever been asked to play Beethoven. I have offered preludes by Debussy as an alternative (he who has always seemed to me to be the lighter and more easily accessible of the two), but no, it has only and ever been Beethoven. This preference I have credited to the evolution and sophistication of the human race. Who enjoy popular music, as long as it's not the most popular. For the rich pride themselves on knowing the pulse of the times—but they must keep ever a heartbeat away from society's tastes. This is what they call fashion.

I wonder if people here even know Beethoven, or Chopin or Debussy. Tomorrow when I meet the symphony orchestra, I will know better. I will, in Agnes' parlance, be able to read the room.

Zipper, 1940

When Zipper arrives at the Manila Metropolitan Theatre and sees it for the first time, he looks at the edifice the way one would remember a first love—how the story moves from glance to touch, from thrill to love; how the present embellishes the past with stepped gables and minarets. But he also sees how the past is native and peculiar to its person. How despite style, there is also substance. He sees this in the wrought-iron gates curled into the plumage of birds of paradise; in the stained glass above it with a design he is being told now by Agnes is a *Javanese batik design, you can see it in the dots and colours and curlicues.*

But to him, after seeing Ermita, and then Intramuros, and then again Ermita, he realizes that The Metropolitan Theatre is indeed Manila. That even with something modern, Manila is also exotic not just to him but also to the people who inhabit it. That perhaps with these strong Filipino flourishes, its people are exoticizing Manila. As an 'exotic' here himself, and seeing the thrall to which he is held as a white man, Zipper understands that the Manila Metropolitan Theatre might be one of the truest expressions of national love.

When he enters the auditorium and hears piano music from the stage, he hears the music float and stay in the lowered wooden arches festooned with bananas and mangoes. He is hearing a prelude by Debussy but he is seeing tropical fruit in a wooden arch. Ever after, that introduction will seem to him a little Eastern.

He is so enthralled by the acoustics that he looks down from the arches to the stage itself. He sees how the orchestra is—at least today—a spare one. There are only two strings, and three percussions, and a grand piano, a flute, and a clarinet; today he sees more of a swing band than an orchestra. In his mind, he calls them respectively, S1, S2, P1, P2, P3, GP, W1, W2. But he has faced sparer orchestras. Not too long ago, all he had was a matchbox and a string.

He looks at the source of the Debussy prelude and sees GP. When she sees him, she stops playing on the keys and stands from the piano seat. He motions for her to resume her seat.

Agnes tells him that the group have all come from the conservatory of the oldest university in Manila—the one they call Santo Tomas after St Thomas the wise.

When he sees the spare orchestra, he asks them if they know the piece *Where or When*. GP nods to him and begins to play the introduction to the Goodman version. He knows it is the Goodman version because GP plays Goodman's piano introduction with aplomb and with a little knowing look in her eye.

Agnes tells Zipper that GP is Alice Feria and that she is from a good family—that she is a musician, yes, but also that she is studying journalism in Santo Tomas. 'A girl like that is likely only scouring the orchestra for a husband,' she tells him. When he gives her a quizzical look, she only tells him that Alice's contemporaries have been married off before the war arrives in the Philippines, and that Alice must want only the same thing.

Alice, Agnes' further tells him, is not the usual GP of the orchestra, she is auditioning for the part, and must pass his assessment before she is promoted. *Although*, Agnes says, most Manila society girls like Chopin and Debussy, and may not share his and Lehman's love for Bach and Beethoven.

Zipper does not know what she means by saying Alice is a Manila society girl but knows by her tone that Agnes means to be pejorative. Zipper, however, knows from the onset that Alice is an artist—whether she is a good or bad one remains to be seen. She is as alive, after all, as much to Debussy as she is to Goodman. He tells this to Agnes, in a voice more forceful than he intends. Further, to Agnes, because he feels that Agnes has been so shortsighted to his fellow musician, he says to her that talent only wants two things, to be fully realized, and to be understood. Agnes furrows her brows at him because she does not understand where all this heat is coming from.

Zipper mellows, does not elaborate on a point he wants to: talent is its own reward and curse, he wants to tell Agnes, but he knows that she would not understand. He knows that when he wants to explain Alice to Agnes, he only wants to explain himself to her, the way he has always felt he has had to explain himself to people like Agnes whom he has known, in all of his society, in all of his life.

Agnes reminds him so much of his mother, especially in this past decade when she has moved into middle age to the first years of old age. Agnes calls him brassy and blusterous when she drops by the symphony sessions but he knows that he can only ever afford to be 'brassy and blusterous' two times every week, and for just the few hours it takes him to train the orchestra. After these spiels, Agnes brings him to a restaurant called Restaurant of Paris in the city—a restaurant run by two expats who Agnes tells him may or may not be American spies.

After their dinners, he takes Agnes home, gives her a pat kiss on the cheek, and then sighs the long sigh of one who is blessedly alone again. When he deposits her to her apartments—there is only obligation to Lehman there, and never any real tenderness—he asks the *kalesa* or the car to drop him off either by the bay, or in any street in the old, walled city of Intramuros. He never really knows who the drivers are in the city; they have either Spanish or American accoutrements.

In Intramuros, and only in Intramuros, does he ever feel at rest. He thinks to himself here are the ancient stones of Manila; here are the secrets whispered by heroes to their paramours; here, they have plotted revolutions by candlelight, in air punctuated by mosquitoes, and harm, and roses.

Ding looks back on the 1936 Olympics in 1940

We were, all ten of us crammed into a small cabin in a ship bound for Paris for some three weeks—some of us had never ridden a boat before and goodness knows I had never been to Europe. Here we were, university boys, bound for the biggest trip of our lives. From Paris, Coach told us that we would catch a train to Berlin.

Paris, we had heard about only from various sweethearts—the wealthiest of whom had fathers who could afford to buy them the latest Parisian fashions from famed ateliers in the city. We'd spent many slow afternoons in their *salas* where they waxed on about the Eiffel Tower, and the books they'd read by French authors—but the thinking girls would summon Rimbaud and Valery and call theirs a friendship that dared not declare its name. I always reasoned that if they had called it a friendship, then a friendship it was, and that friendship was its only name.

Each time I said this to a group of otherwise thoughtful and sweet girls, they would go into a tittering frenzy. Bewildered,

I only left their company for girls less opinionated. In soirees, this usually meant the shy and reserved ones, coughing at their first cigarettes in dark loveseats. More and more these days, it meant Linang, neither shy nor tittering, standing apart and drawing on one of her father's cigarettes; assessing everyone in the room coolly, a kind of smile on her face, a kind of arch in the brow that one would only know to be mocking if one truly knew her. Otherwise, her manners were perfect, her laugh polite, her wit fast.

During those feverish weeks at sea, where we seemed always to be sick with something, the sea itself or the idea of home, it was always good to carry the memory of one of these girls close at hand. It was almost as if we were going off to war somehow, and that the memory of these girls made us remember we were men. We talked not so much of liberties taken as we did liberties we would be allowed to take once we returned home as heroes. This did not mean that we were expected to win—rather, our adventures overseas would have given us the shine of a new breed of hero: the well-travelled and cosmopolitan Filipino man. At least to the impressionable young girls in our circles. Compare us to the other boys who had been left behind, and there was absolutely no match and no game. It had always seemed like an unfair fight to me—I can almost hear Linang talk about her less remarkable suitors and proclaiming that compared to us, it was as if they brought knives to a gun fight.

It had all seemed so glamorous in the telling—three weeks at sea to Paris, and then Berlin where only the single-most important event in all our lives awaited us. That trip, in and of itself, would have been the biggest adventure of our lives, that much remained clear.

It was part of my Jesuit education to hope for great things but not to expect anything. This gave me a certain quietness of temper, a certain moderation of heart, that made me play well on the court even if the opposing team seemed out for blood. This did not make me team captain like Padilla, or co-team captain like Cruz, both of whom exuded a kind of greatness on the court. By their stance and fire on and off it, respectively and conversely, one always believed they were meant for importance. I do not think I was meant for importance, and so joy happens to me faster and more immediately than it does to the other boys on the team. I have never been haunted by who I might be in the future; my game has always been consistent.

Every time I tell this story to whoever will listen—from that first wide-eyed and enraptured audience, and then, over the years, to a trickled-down crowd of old-timers and sports veterans—no one has ever asked me what we have achieved in the long days since. Berlin would forever be our crowning achievement to any local audience. If the looming war would make us heroes or husbands, if the next decades would make us statesmen or senators, then these were not the dreams everyone wanted to hear, these were not the stories they wrote about in newspapers. They did not expect us to have dreams beyond Berlin, and they did not dream anything else for us.

If Paris was familiar to us—the way perfume is familiar as second-hand information, then Berlin was like the Spanish I dream in, without knowing anything but a smattering of phrases. I only know Spanish in curse and greeting. I know Spanish the way Linang knows French—conversationally, and confident in that conversation only when very, very lit. Berlin was like that Spanish. Something both distant and real.

I did not know that upon reaching Paris, we would be thrust into the smallest cabin in the train to Berlin. I did not know that we would arrive in Berlin to a blitz of flashbulbs. I did not know that I would experience the same kind of otherness

I experienced from the Americans back home, who eyed us local boys with a kind of sneering superiority.

They were not a majority back home and so one always learned to brush off any hard feelings from the few encounters we'd had, and the slight scrapes that managed to bruise the ego harder than the skin. But otherness in Berlin was inescapable. Never have I ever felt as adored or as disdained.

We belonged to a team called the Pacific Islanders, which gave us an exoticism I thought was better reserved for actual islanders in our country, and not boys from Manila with American tastes and educations. But we had to be called something that subscribed to a universal notion of the Pacific islander; perhaps a people who had just discovered shoes in the past decade, and who still drank out of coconut husks.

Leading up to our games, we received perfumed letters from what to us was the most exotic thing in the world: the blonde, Teutonic girl. When we received such letters, often done in stiff and unwieldy English (and overly scented with lavender or vanilla or anis), it made us feel seven feet tall; as though we'd snatched jump balls over our white contemporaries who were easily a foot taller than us. The letters made us float on air—until we were ushered into a restaurant and given the table at the back, either beside the kitchen or beside the water closet.

The games themselves were a difficult animal. There were rules imposed on us that seemed almost whimsical. All of us islanders were roughly the same height—tall by Filipino standards but miniscule by Western ones. Prior to this, we had only ever competed with fellow Filipinos of the same build and height. The games conformed to the basketball rules we knew—that the jump ball was ours after every basket was made. This only made sense, and was ostensibly only fair, if all the players were of the same height. In Berlin, our opponents were close to six and a half feet, some close to seven, which meant that the rules did not apply fairly to us. Still, we fought like dogs and placed fifth overall in those skewed Olympics. The win itself felt bittersweet—it was as if we were the ones who had brought knives to a gun fight and had miraculously somehow put up a good fight, even if we had lost the game. When I returned home, we loomed as largely over the local boys—as though we'd gone shadowboxing with them, and they were the flesh, and we were the dark titans on the wall. For we were versions of each other, I suppose, either the worst or the best.

I knew I had changed, but I didn't know how much I had, until I saw Linang the Saturday after we arrived. If she had assessed me coolly as a prospect, that coolness had somehow turned into a kind of ardour. She had never looked so feminine, and I had only then noticed her own perfume—not her mother's scent which had punctuated the air with sharp flowers, but something less cloying and more suited to the Manila air it inhabited. She did not smell like those letters I had kept folded in my trousers pocket, letters that mother washed until the ink stained my pockets almost permanently: Teutonic ink betraying a Teutonic English, and tattooing my Filipino trousers with an almost historical bittersweetness.

Linang smelled like *jasmin*. She had received me in the Balintawak style common to ladies whose families had vacation homes away from Manila. She received me as a gentle Filipina woman would, whose sweetheart had just returned from the very arms of Europe, literally and figuratively. She did not compete with some European girl a lesser local girl would have marked in her mind as a rival to my affections; she came to me as a peerless contrast. Perhaps it was a measured move, but it had seemed like the absolute right one. She had made me feel like I had really and truly come home.

Perhaps, this was a home my father had dreamed for himself one generation before me. When that seemed unattainable, he had dreamed it for me, and now here I was, a local hero, gathered into the good graces of a good girl from a good Manila family.

It was at that moment that Linang had first seemed beautiful to me, and that she seemed peerless. It was at that moment that I saw how I might love her, and it was at that moment that I saw in her eyes how she might love me.

It was only a matter of time when those looks we proffered as lovers could be proven wrong—we could not have known then what the years had in store for us. In hindsight, the cards in the deck were having a good laugh; they were content taking us as fools.

Ding, 1940

I had it in my mind to tell Macario that I wished to court Linang that afternoon. Comely and intimidating Linang whose wit could draw my breath, and whose conversation could draw on all my academic resources in a single afternoon—she knew Rilke and Rodin, but she also knew Rizal, and Villa, and Manalang-Gloria. I would never be bored by Linang, but she might be bored by me in a few years' time. And so, I decided, it was that day or never.

I had been giving myself man-to-man talks for days, or should I say man-to-self talks, and had made up my mind and unmade it several times—but that day would be different, I told myself. Only, the cutting and otherwise smartly calculating Linang had chosen that very day to introduce me to Alice Feria.

When I am received in the Callao sala, Alice and Linang are seated by the Steinway playing a piece that requires two players—I do not catch the full melody but from the girlish laughter, I know that it is not a serious piece. Macario leans against the piano top, *Blue Moon* he sings, exaggeratedly, *you saw me standing alone.* And then I catch his eye, and the singing stops but the song goes on.

'Why hello there, Ding,' Macario says winking at me. I see Linang nudge Alice. And then she turns from the piano seat to greet me. *I see the guest of dishonour is here*, she says, laughingly, kissing my cheek. Alice turns from the piano. *Guest of dishonour,* Linang says, *meet guest of honour, Alice Feria.*

I see her small eyes are hazel and that her thin lids draw sharply down their edges. Ringlets of light brown hair are drawn from her forehead by hairpins while larger curls fall to her nape. While she stands from the seat, she smiles at me shyly, and does not reach out a hand. She says at least, to me, gently: *How do you do, Ding? I've heard a lot about you.*

Good things I hope, I say, expectedly.

Mostly good things, she says. When she sees my confusion, she amends her forwardness.

I'm kidding, Ding. I've heard only good things. She reaches out her right hand and something comes over me that I think she means for me to kiss the back of it. And so, I draw the hand and brush it quickly with my lips. Her white, moon-shaped face reddens.

I think she only meant for you to shake her hand, Ding, Linang says laughingly. *I mean, you've only just met—don't you think it's a little too soon for a kiss?* I am so undone by my behaviour that Linang takes my hand and draws me to the sofa. *There, there, Ding. Take a seat. You're paler than an Americano.*

I notice that the two are similarly dressed but that Linang's dress is green, and Alice's blue, and that Linang has chosen coral earrings, but that Alice wears pearls.

Play us something Alice, Linang says. I am still so caught in my embarrassment that I do not notice how for the first time Linang is holding on to my hand longer than is appropriate. *Alice plays Chopin the way my father plays the President,* Linang says, wryly.

'Linang,' Macario warns. At first, I think this is because Linang has said something unflattering about both her father and the President. But after he speaks, Linang withdraws her hand from mine.

And then Alice plays—broken chords on her left hand, keeping steady time—her right hand fluttering first like a fan and then like wings. I have never heard the piece but I feel strangely nostalgic when I hear it. In Alice's hands, the afternoon is an air, a dream.

The sunlight coming in through the white tiles on the windows feels obscure and warm. Where the windows part, the warmth of a late Manila afternoon strikes the hood of the piano, and Alice's hands, rendering them so white, I can see the blue-green veins sliding from her knuckles to the tops of her wrists.

We hear the prattle and laughter of the help in the kitchen, the first hiss of dinner. Mr Callao will be returning home from work shortly, and already the house anticipates him; and when he enters the foyer, his slippers will be waiting for him. Mrs Callao will pour him a drink and when he enters the sala, it will be piano music that greets him. I want to live forever in that house at that moment, anticipating Mr Callao's arrival, and in the swell of Alice's nocturne.

The house is not a church but it has never felt so holy; nor has the present felt so completely symmetrical on that street and in that house; and when we hear Mr Callao's car coming up the drive, and then his feet stride into the sala, there is a peace so complete, my heart feels like it might break. And then I see Macario looking at Alice as if through my eyes, and then I see Macario looking at me looking at Alice as if through his. And then I see Linang running into her father's arms, as if he was a buoy and she was drowning.

1941

On our wedding day, Alice, I have not seen a more radiant human being. You would not appreciate my saying 'wife' or 'woman' but you do appreciate the more sweeping assignation. You are a radiant human being.

It is a small wedding because you keep such a small circle. Here is your father, come from the provinces, and here is your adoptive mother who is as crude as a wooden slipper. Here is my snob of a friend, Edilberto, who fancies himself a 'moving-pictures director,' but who cannot abide Filipinos coming into the theatre in their *bakyas*. He laughs at Salvacion, who he calls rich *bakya*. Salvacion doesn't even wear bakyas, but Edilberto is too myopic to see this. He has been wearing blinders since birth.

Here are my father and my mother, and my little sister Nenang. My father wears his Americano with its tie and bowler hat like an old *ilustrado*; here is my mother with her *traje de mestiza*, and here is my sister Nenang in her smart sailor's dress. 'We have at our wedding, the entire history of Philippine colonization,' you had whispered.

You have only invited your father, and your adoptive mother and your new friend, Pilar. None of your old friends—and none of mine—is here, but that is of no importance when I think of the most confounding mystery of my life: *you chose me*. Out of all the men you could have chosen. And that by turns bewilders and scares me. I am nothing, these days, if not grateful.

When your father and Salvacion approach my father and mother for what they call *cuentas claras;* when our wedding to them means nothing more than splitting nickels and dimes, pesos and centavos, I look at you and think that you are not of this world, that there are things not of this world that make themselves known here, in this world's low and imperious corners. And I am yours now, as much as you are mine.

8 December 1941

At three in the morning, US Navy channels from Hawaii sent fleet commander Rear Admiral Thomas C. Hart a message: AIR RAID AT PEARL HARBOR—THIS IS NO DRILL. Reports have it that Hart who detested his superior, MacArthur, had failed to bring him the news. MacArthur was only informed forty minutes later by his chief of staff, Major General Richard K. Sutherland, who had not received the message, but had heard it on the radio.

Shortly, the General received a call from Brigadier General Leonard T. Gerow, all the way from Washington. Gerow had warned him to prepare for a Japanese strike against the Philippines given the great damage done at Pearl Harbor. MacArthur will later go on to say that the call he received from Gerow had only insinuated that 'Japan had suffered a setback.' In truth, the Japanese are astonished to discover how easy it has been to enter Manila. Minutes after Pearl Harbor, their aircraft can be heard flying over the city.

Just a few hours before, Alice had been explaining to Ding that she is certain about Chopin and Debussy for tomorrow's audition for Zipper. He will want her to play Beethoven, but Beethoven requires stamina and she does not like his darkness, even in his sonatas.

She tells Ding that she is to start with a nocturne by Chopin, and then a prelude by Debussy, and then a sonata by Beethoven—that she is surest of Chopin, that her favourite is Debussy, but that she is sure that it is Beethoven Zipper most wants to hear her play. He has been making the orchestra practice Eroica for weeks now; so much so that Alice believes he will want her to play a piece by his favourite composer.

When Ding asks her about this Chopin nocturne, he sees Alice's eyes turn serious. He sees her eyes think of how to translate music to a layman. She tells him that the piece has one form but two ideas and a coda. She tells him that the two ideas in the music have three phrases—phrase one being the melody and phrase two being the melody with embellishments. So she plays the third phrase—the second idea of the nocturne she explains; the steadiness of her left hand anchoring the flight of her right. This is the phrase Chopin indicates should be played suddenly and softly—*as with all the movements in my life, Ding*, she had said, *some more sudden than soft*—

Ding, 1941

It is the neighbour Will Fernandez who comes into our home running and saying have you heard the news, have you heard the news? He said it was the Americans and Japanese duking it out on Corregidor and Bataan. I had been loathe to assign a provenance to such attacks—Bataan was five to six hours away from Manila by car, and Corregidor two hours by boat, and I had not wanted to unsettle this momentary calm by assigning trouble from two separate directions; trouble that would come inevitably to Manila—it was only a question of when, and from which direction. Direction alone could dictate time.

Instead, I told Alice that the sounds sounded like some kind of doom music—that Manila was a piece awaiting its name and that the music was happening elsewhere. I asked Alice to name the music as though it were a symphony. What piece would it be, and by which composer?

She told me that it seemed like a symphony scored for bassoons and horns—the horns being from Corregidor and the bassoons from Bataan, although the sounds we heard were likely coming from Corregidor; Bataan's upheavals were too far away.

Manila, Alice continued, would be waiting in the wings. If this were a symphony, Manila, she said, would be the strings, and would only come in in the second movement. It was clear Alice was composing the battle sounds into a kind of crazed music in her mind.

There is my symphony Ding, she said, laughingly, *there is my final audition. You see it was never Debussy or Chopin. Here, before us, is the Beethoven Zipper always wanted me to play.*

Part Four

Manila, 1942

Zipper, 1942

Alice, I soon learn, is not part of the orchestra. She is merely substituting for Toto Fernandez, who has been indisposed since I have arrived. That is the public statement. Private murmurs have it that he is part of the resistance movement against the Japanese, and that he is being held in a dungeon in the walled city. One that is called by the name of a saint whose mercies and conditions of beautification I am strangely familiar with: *Santa Barbara*. Saint Barbara, the patron saint of gunpowder and those who die without the rites of their faith.

Though I do not know the exact location of this *baluarte*, I am acquainted with the famous walled city that stands on its dark feet. I have walked many nights on its cobblestoned streets, and taken in its very flavors and scents. It is contemporaneous with many of Europe's best cities, but it is old by new world standards. I know that this walled city is more than three hundred years old—that its forts were erected against Chinese pirates that threatened Spanish rule. And that it was a port once upon a time, carrying gold and porcelain to Acapulco. This trade had enriched the Spanish and their allies in this town.

Agnes would have me believe that Filipinos are inherently trusting and guileless, and that it is by virtue of these attributes that they were taken advantage of. But I also know that there are people called Toto Fernandez who are taken to underground dungeons in the underbelly of the city. Rumour has it that in these underground tunnels, water from the Pasig river swells at high tide to meet the bay, and that it is made to drown guerillas and spies in the underground dungeon.

I have known many godless places in my life and know that it is usual for ungodly things to happen in sacred spaces, sometimes named for Christian saints.

Agnes tells me that the Philippines has been so used to its feudal systems that it has always needed a landlord. That the Philippines is one big feudal parlour, and that they cannot rule themselves as the west has always ruled itself. She has not known Dachau or Buchenwald as I have known Dachau and Buchenwald. She simply sees herself as a Jewess in Manila, as privileged as a white woman might be in Manila. As light of skin as the very first missionaries who approached these shores at the turn of the century. In the Philippines, she is not a Jew. She is a white woman whose lineage has not yet caught up with her. Even the Americans treat her as they would their own despite her Jewish-European accent. Manileños cannot see beyond her fair skin and her light hair. But I *know*. I know. And knowing, I cannot go about my way as blithely as she does, and in such foreign shores as these.

I know there is a town in America called Santa Barbara—that it is the haven for the very rich. Perhaps there is a Jew in that town called Santa Barbara, as well as there is a Jew in the Philippines who by the looks of it must escape in some way a dungeon named after her.

Saigo, 1942

They talk of guerillas in Manila—Filipinos and Americans who would rather flee to the boondocks or monitor Japanese affairs and disclose them to their leader MacArthur via radio. These people could be everyday Filipinos or American expats. I have heard that the Jew, Zipper, conductor of the Manila Symphony Orchestra is one such guerilla. I had gotten a dispatch from headquarters to monitor his actions. I know now that twice a week he conducts the Manila Symphony Orchestra at the Metropolitan Theatre in Manila. I had taken to some shadow-play in those months and had hidden myself in the theatre's dark corners. But it was not during those moments that I heard of Zipper's plans.

I had heard instead from an informant that Zipper had told the orchestra that we had wanted them to play victorious songs for the benefit of our victory over the Americans, as well as for our own imperial glory. Zipper had said that he would not give us the satisfaction of hearing Manila's best orchestra play.

I had also heard from this informant that Zipper has hatched a plan to bury all their instruments. He has told them that rather than acquiesce to the Japanese, he will pretend that the orchestra members have all left the orchestra to attend to more important matters, such as their families and livelihoods. He has told them to bury their respective instruments in their backyards so that they will not play for the Japanese.

Ding, 1942

I have never buried a single thing in my life. And so, when Alice tells me that Zipper has asked her to bury her practice piano, the idea is not only preposterous to me, it also challenges my notion of what a man should be able to carry and bear. For I will bear Alice's many whims and moods which sometimes weigh on me with as much heft and load as this piano itself. I bear this like a patient man who has read his bible, and who has chosen the Corinthians for his wedding vow. Her emotional weight I have been ready for, prepared of all people by Linang who constantly complained to me about Alice's many colours— there were her blues, which meant a melancholy easily lifted by music or books; and then there were her yellows (a kind of honey, a kind of mustard, Linang had offered, never undiminished like noon) which could cheer anybody in the room. And then, of course, there were her reds—her reds which could last for days, and which no amount of cheering could chase away. It had only to run its course, which could take anywhere between three days and five.

I suspect that no amount or persuasion can sway Alice not to bury this piano—a *Chassaigne Frère*—an elegant piece of wood that hasn't quite reached the reputation of the Steinway that many of Manila's elite keep in their *salas*. But it is a beautiful piano nonetheless and I am inordinately loathe to dig it an early grave.

I do not know the first thing about dismantling a piano, but I am a man who knows where places fit and fold. I know instinctively to dismantle the legs, which makes Alice proclaim that I have a future as a mover after the war. Legs dismantled— some trouble with the pedal, some screw too tightly corked into the wood—I tie them all together with rope. I tell Alice that this piano should only momentarily be buried, and that we must ease it into the earth with softness and delicacy. Alice suggests wrapping the main body in blankets to protect it from damage, and to protect anything else that might be buried along with it. Alice reminds me to mind the top of the piano best, where its most delicate parts are. She means the strings, but I also know she is remembering all the music she has played on its keys—music the strings have wavered into the air of many slow afternoons with a kind of evangelic turning. For Alice has converted me to music with this very piano. We wrap its main bulk with two thick coverlets, and tie the top to its bottom with rope.

After the piano is wrapped, I ask the neighbour Will Fernandez to help me dig its temporary grave. It takes us a day and a half since we cannot dig too deep. Alice has given us two days to sort it out, and we do it. I carry Alice's weight, and I do it.

Alice, 1942

When she sees the man through the window in his olive-green uniform, she knows that he is not a typical Japanese officer. Although he is dressed as a cavalry officer, he has a white band around his left arm with two red characters. She will later understand this to mean *ken* and *hei,* law and soldier.

He raps on their door with a bamboo sword.

Alice takes a second to answer, squares her shoulders. She has been preparing herself for something like this to happen and yet it still catches her by surprise. She sees a young soldier with eyes that could almost be the eyes of her relatives in Iloilo only they squint at her superciliously.

'It has been told to me that you have buried your piano so that you will not play for the glory of the empire,' the man says.

'No, that is not true, Officer. I am only the wife of a citizen of Manila. I sometimes play for the Manila Symphony Orchestra, yes, but that is only to substitute for Toto Fernandez, their main pianist.'

'Who is it, Alice?' asks Ding from within the house.

'Just a kind Japanese soldier, Ding,' she answers sweetly. 'He has come to see how we are faring.'

'Show me to the backyard,' Saigo tells Alice.

'But there is nothing in the backyard, officer. Only mud and brown grass we have not been able to make live this past year.'

'Show me to the backyard,' Saigo growls, taps his bamboo stick on his left palm.

Alice leads him to the garden and Saigo sees it is all well but for a small plot whose slightly upturned edges suggest a new bulge. Ding follows them there and Saigo tells him to begin digging. He has not gone five inches into the dirt when Saigo sees the curved edges of a massive instrument wrapped in a blanket. It is Alice's piano.

'Why bury the piano?' Saigo asks her.

'It has gotten to be too much to care for,' she says. 'One must oil the strings, and polish the wood, and I'm afraid we do not have enough money for its upkeep.'

'This is a piano and you play for the Manila Symphony Orchestra, yes?'

'Yes,' she acquiesces.

'You will not play for Japanese?'

'No, it is not like that the officer. We cannot afford to keep our instruments—we who have lost our livelihoods during the occupation—we—'

'Enough. Come with me.'

'Where are you taking her?' Ding shouts from the shadows. 'Where are you taking my wife?'

Saigo notes how Ding Obordo eyes him with the same malicious intent as other Filipinos do when they see him in the street. Saigo remembers how they salute him, but they do so mockingly, with a little sneer on their faces, a little malice in the eyes.

Saigo assesses Ding's bearing—the slight frame, the camisa de chino, the trousers hitched to just above the ankles. The clothes are faded, but these are the clothes Saigo has seen on local gentlemen. Saigo looks at him disdainfully and thinks to himself that Ding must have soft hands.

It pierces him that such a man could protect a guerilla when he should be allying himself with Saigo, a protector of Asia, a soldier not just of the empire, but of the very race itself. At this very moment, he does not hate anyone in this world as much as he hates Ding. He feels a wild quiver in his eye. He draws his hand to his pistol.

'No,' says Alice. 'No, officer. Please. Please.'

Saigo grazes the trigger in his pocket, draws the gun to his hand, and hits Ding sideways with the brass. Alice screams, then wails, then cries. There is no sound more grating to Saigo in the entire world.

He does not give her enough time to attend to her husband or to appraise the damage he has done to his skull—he grabs her arm and prises her soft flesh as though it were her throat and not her arm. He knows he will leave marks tomorrow. Proud, wild marks the colour of berries.

He will take her where he has taken so many other guerillas. To the darkness of the underbelly itself.

Saigo, 1942

In this dank dungeon, in these dark times, I am happy knowing only that those who are traitors to the cause suffer slow deaths. Then and only then do I feel entirely alive. When the desk officer sees me take a *gentlewoman* to the dungeons, I see the slow smile on his lips. 'No woman or child safe from you, eh, officer?' he says.

I do not care if his tone is mocking. When he looks up from his deskwork and sees Alice Feria Obordo's face, he gives me a hard, penetrating look. 'Surely this is a gentlewoman,' he says. 'Surely you are mistaken.' His bland gaze shows his contempt.

I tell him that I have been monitoring this woman for close to a year—that I have long suspected her of being part of the resistance. I tell him that any doubt I may have had about the truth of my beliefs has been tested by monitoring her movements. I tell him that my knowledge of this woman is infallible.

He is still not swayed. 'Are you sure this woman hasn't just spurned you?' he says with a laugh in his eyes. 'Are you mocking me, officer?' I say, ready to draw my gun. He only shakes his head, and nods for me to follow him to a crowded cell, packed to its bars with dirty and emaciated guerilla fighters.

Tomorrow's high tide from the river will flood this dungeon, drowning every brown and white guerilla in its wake. Tomorrow, they, as Alice, will forget who they live for, and what they fight for, releasing themselves, finally, into their last lungful of water.

* * *

Because Zipper has connections who remain unattainable to me as kempeitai, I do not know who has hidden him. If they are from the American ranks and not from Filipino ones, he will have been doubly kept protected from me. I know that for her insult to the empire, and as a Filipino, Alice will not have as much weight as the mastermind of her crime. But I must content myself with the knowledge that I have apprehended everything that she stands for, even if she is but a small cog in the teeth of a greater machine.

I know that at best, Zipper will be taken to a Manila precinct and not a dungeon such as this one. But I do not have control over such events. I have only control of Alice, and Alice in her wild fear no longer has any control over herself.

I believe that Alice is, as the officer has appraised her, a gentlewoman. Under normal circumstances, I would have gladly ushered her back into the proud poverty of her Manila life. A life of rations and prayers. And music, when rations and prayers do not quite prove enough for survival.

But these are not normal circumstances. War is the great equalizer, if not to its great men, then to the people they govern. If not to emperors and generals, then to common men. As an officer of the Japanese empire, I alone have might—so much of it during these times that I might as well be emperor and general, consigned to this earth by heaven and imperial dictum.

In this light, no matter her former power or wealth or prestige, I am finally more powerful than Alice and all Filipinos who are like Alice, and all Filipinos who are not like Alice, but who look at me with the same suspicion and disdain.

When I think of this, I feel a bright surge in my ears. I do not understand such loyalty to a colonial master—this master who has brought the worst of its subjects to consort with the best of them. A colonial master who marries its commoners to their noble women. 'They bring their worst to marry our best,' is something I myself have heard Alice whisper to the women in the orchestra.

It so confounds me that it gives me a kind of joy to wait out Alice's last hours with her in this dungeon. Indeed, all things that have confounded me since I was first stationed in this country three years ago will ease themselves soon enough into happy oblivion. And it will be here—all that evening out of every hard emotion I have felt since I first set foot upon these shores.

I will stay until the very last minute I must go to save myself.

* * *

It is high noon now. In a few short hours, I will release myself back into the air of Intramuros and feel the throb and swell of water beneath my feet. When I do, then I know that it is done. With these traitors, I drown all the humiliations I have suffered since I first set foot on these shores. I drown out all the sneers of its gentlemen and oligarchs. I drown out the withdrawn hands of commoners I have bent to shake. I drown out the spit of that washerwoman when I addressed her mistress in the street.

I do not care that I have to suffer the dank air of this dungeon for this. I do not care if I misplace the hour and that I myself am caught in the first swell before I run up the stone steps to save myself. It will be done—and so will everyone here who is caught by the tide at its high hour.

The water will come for their ankles and then their knees. And then for their necks. It will wash them until it seeps into their lungs. It will come for them and I will be here to witness it. I will be here to witness the very first swell of it.

Saigo

I hear footsteps bound down the mossy stones and instinctively, my hand draws to my gun. It isn't until I hear a voice speaking in my tongue consort tentatively with the dungeon master, that my hand and heart ease.

The man introduces himself as a Captain of the Imperial Army. When our eyes meet, he looks at me with a contempt in his eyes that I do not understand. He narrows his eyes on me with more hatred than any one I have seen in my life, even on these shores. And then he makes as though he does not recognize me, and turns so sharply away I might as well be the enemy.

He bids the dungeon master come. His eyes scour the dungeon once then twice. Then once then twice again until it seems he has seen every face in that cell that must contain more than a hundred guerillas. He scours the cell again and again until I see the moment their eyes meet.

Alice, tentative. Alice whose eyes hunger has made soft and sharp at the same time by gaslight. And then the captain's eyes that are so clear and soft now, I think he must have been either a poet or a teacher. The captain smiles at Alice wanly.

She recognizes him but her mouth draws back into a small smile this time, as though they keep a secret between them. A secret not delicious but deep.

'Do you know this woman?' the dungeon master says. The captain answers, 'She is only a woman whose father's garden I tended a long way north before we arrived. She was always kind to me. I am quite sure she has been mistaken as someone else by some mistaken source.' Quickly, he turns to the dungeon master. 'We have, among our ranks, several mistaken sources who only want to please those higher-ranking.' The dungeon master looks at me knowingly then shakes his head. 'I understand, officer,' he tells the captain.

The captain does not even give me a second look. He simply points to Alice and tells the dungeon master to release her. The chorus of guerillas in the cell ripens to a grating pitch. 'Me!' yells a small chorus. 'Me!' yells another and another. But it appears that the captain doesn't hear anything. He points only at Alice and tells the dungeon master, 'Her. Only her.' As the dungeon master pulls out his key, the soldier clicks his heels and bows to his fellow soldier. And then he bounds up the steps as quickly as he came.

Haruki, 1942

And so I know now why you have happened to my life, and I have happened to yours. And so I know now what I have always needed to do. Do you know, Alice, that I had never so much as seen a rose up close until Callao's garden—that I had to pretend I was a specialist, tending them, in what would be the most outrageous charade of my life?

I had drenched Callao's roses with too much water the first month in Baguio. They had wilted so much then, their petals folding in like the hands of a courtesan in those stories my mother told me about all those years we were hungry. I had watered them twice a day then. They'd grown spotted and dank with something I later learned was mildew.

It was Tentay, watching me solemnly from a window for the better part of a month, who had given me peat and compost to mix in with the soil. It was also she who told me that bushes only needed watering once a day. I'd known their quirks on the second month. Do not water the foliage, point the watering pot directly at the soil. Only on the third month did the roses thrive. And it was then that we met.

When the officers told me they had seen Saigo, gentlewoman in tow, march to the dungeon in the walled city, I had only the slightest suspicion it would be you. I had felt that suspicion in the gut where I had only felt it one other time in my life. I had felt it the day my father disappeared into the swells of the water he loved.

Even then, such feelings ran counter to all the outward signs. There was a high sun when I said goodbye to my father, not knowing that it would be the last time. It was a high sun that I took to be an auspicious sign that he would return.

When I heard that Saigo had taken a woman into the bowels of the walled city, there was the same light I had seen that day with my father. Nothing outwardly amiss. Only amiss was a single kick, small as a sigh, in the gut.

I always knew Saigo was a vengeful man—such was his reputation with his kind, and with us soldiers. This propensity had turned him small and petty. Any woman he had seen fit to persecute would have been a woman important to him in some way. My first guess was that it was a woman he had wanted his way with, and who had spurned him, and had knotted up his insides, and turned his mind animal. I have seen it with many men who had come with me to these shores. I had heard reports that Saigo had been tormenting the old proprietor of Restaurant de Paris— that he had brought two Filipina prostitutes to the place. The proprietor had refused to charge him. But, Saigo had demanded to be charged. When the bill came, he had charged the owner with insubordination and threatened to bring her to Fort Santiago. He had waved his pistol around recklessly, but he had met more than his match with this woman. The woman had had her wits about her and had called headquarters to report on Saigo's recklessness and drinking. She had known that there was a code of conduct expected of Japanese soldiers—no soldier could imbibe alcohol while on duty; further, no subject of the imperial army had the power to intimidate or hurt civilians. Saigo had slunk away then before he could be apprehended or punished.

Long story short, I had made up my mind that whoever Saigo had a bone to pick with was a woman who needed my saving. I could not have known then that that woman was you. My quick stride to the dungeon, on little more than a suspicion, did not involve you, though I had it in my mind that it might involve someone like you.

When I had seen your face—your one true face and not the face I had seen only in memory or in dreams this past year. When I had seen your one true face. And not the imagined face I was always afraid time would rub false, or break from its symmetry like the noses of saints in your cathedrals here, like the hands of saints in your cathedrals and shrines here. When I had seen your one true face. Not the face I had feared my mind had remembered falsely so that your eyes seemed darker than they are, or your chin more round than square, or your nose wider than upturned.

When I had seen your one true face, at that moment between life and death, it was the face I had imagined all these months. It became clear that you were as real in my mind as you were actual in my eyes. So well do I know you. I had not realized it until then.

With a single look, at that moment between life and death, you had made perfect all my seasons. You had laved my dirt with sun and rain, just so. The stones in the garden had fallen into place then, and the sun struck a sudden flush of petals with just the right bend of light. And all the long necks of roses kissed the air. And you made me a perfect form with a single look— you had designed me into a perfect order, into a perfect garden.

And I will never be so arranged again, and I will not see you again, and fare you well, and goodbye, Alice. Alice.

Ding, 1942

It was the neighbour who had found me, unconscious after the *kempeitai* officer who had appeared to know Alice had left me for dead when he took her. I am thankful that I slipped into a deep sleep then for it had kept me from worrying about her, and fearing she had been taken to her death in some dungeon that smelled of shit and piss; it had kept me from thinking that she might have been split with a saber by the very butcher of Fort Santiago himself. Had the blow been softer, had I sustained only a minor injury, my mind would have raced to many unforgiving places. I would have imagined Alice compromised, stripped, badly touched, or summarily killed. I am glad I was closer to death than I was to life—if not vitally than in consciousness. Many unthinkable things had happened to people who had been close to us. Linang had had the misapprehension that nothing untoward could ever happen to her class—to her family and her kin least of all, who had ties to the government, and who glided easily into the foyers of the upper-middle class. She had always told me that if I stuck to her side, I would be invincible because class always stuck to class, and class would always look out for fellow class. Linang must have been instructed only by her father's upper-middle class view—I was not, individually, middle class, and Alice was upper middle class only by way of new money. Our union, at best, could only be middle class—a step below, perhaps, from the echelons of society Linang was born into, and which she always took for granted. It was privilege that kept her safe and blind to the rest of the world. She could never be blamed for it, and she never had to fight for it. It was hers by birthright, where the rest of its aspirants had to fight tooth and nail for it, as my father had in his time.

I knew that by class alone, Alice and I should have been kept safe from the intrusion of the Japanese. Had I married a less impassioned girl, I would have been less in love than I was with Alice. Alice who had a kind of national pride I had never seen in Linang; a kind of patriotism that had kept her striving for a life beyond our comfortable hearth and home. Linang would have kept me comfortable. She would have ensconced me in an encompassing warm web of class by association. Had I married Linang, only time would have launched me into the grudging arms of Manila society as my father had always hoped. But I did not love Linang—I loved Alice, and despite his outward disapproval, I know that my father had silently approved of the match.

Alice may not be old rich but she is new rich, and if that is not the same thing, given the changing course of history, it is almost the same thing. I had thought that the small difference between the two would have kept us safe from the Japanese. Alice had no connections and no pedigree. Her mother and father were not kissing cousins; they did not know any presidents, they did not receive any heads of state in their *sala*. Anyone would have thought that we could sink into the everyday strife

of everyday Filipinos who had found themselves casualties of
petty and easy crimes during the occupation—but Alice had
a rebellious streak that kept us always on the brink of almost
certain trouble.

It was common knowledge now that the Japanese went for
the upper class—they did this to prominent families, shelling
their houses with bombs, cutting their bodies in two with
their knives, leaving them for dead, or crazed enough to wish
they were dead. I can only guess that they had suspected their
patriarchs to have had close ties and unending loyalty to the
Americans—or that their sons were part of the United States
Armed Forces of the Philippines, which many, but not all, were.
Perhaps many of them were like me, groveling for the approval
of the upper class all their lives, by turns condescended on and
politely disdained. Skill and talent had got me into their inner
graces, but I was not a troublesome boy. I was not quarrelsome:
I was grateful. And I was not of another race. I could have
chosen not to be conscripted into a small eastern chapter of an
American war.

Not too far elsewhere were boys who did not have the same
choices I did. Put in a boy of my class from an enemy country
and you could be sure that all hell would break loose. Dogs of
war, and all that. Linang would have quoted Shakespeare, but
here Alice lives it. I know Linang must be safe with her Ermita
connections, but here Alice and I are merely *nouveau*, to borrow
a term Linang has often used to describe Alice; and we should
be safe, but Alice has courted trouble, whether she means to or
not.

When I had come to, Alice was in the room with me—
spared by some miracle from certain death in Fort Santiago.
She had nursed me, alternately with the good Fernandezes, until
it had been agreed that we could move safely into our house.

Salvacion, 1942

With Alice happily married to Ding—however long this happiness will last is God's good guess because I know Alice; there is a relative calm to the girl now when there was only a kind of nervous energy to her in days past. There is the blush of new wifehood in her face now, when there was always the smallest cast of sadness in her eyes. Even on her good and generous days, which she glided through with perfect equanimity and grace.

She is playing the piano less and less these days, which I will take as a good sign. When I visit her conjugal home in Malate, near enough to my home to merit more than the occasional visit, she receives me easily and talks of learning the recipes she grew up with so that she might 'whip them up for Ding.' She has taken to speaking in American idioms it takes me a hard second to understand. ''Whip them up' means I am going to quickly recreate them in the kitchen, mama,' she says, reading my mind. Prior to that, I had thought she meant that she would literally whip the cubes of beef, and potatoes and carrots to a sad mash. I had thought she would annihilate the cabbage and the eggplant to

132

a pulp. That was no way to treat my mother's *puchero*, I thought, that had gained small fame for its sumptuousness, at least in our district. But now I learned that to whip something up meant graces in the kitchen—a miracle because Alice never learned to cook.

If I am honest, perhaps Alice hasn't taken to her music because the piano is not in playing shape, thanks to Zipper and all his guerilla ideas. Alice had thought it best to hide this fact from me but the neighbours talk, and their talk glides easily down the grapevine in our small, insular district. It is so small as to almost be incestuous.

I now know that Alice's former conductor Zipper had asked the members of his symphony orchestra to bury their instruments before the Japanese attacks came full throttle to Manila. I did not think that Alice would take part in such foolishness (tomfoolery, Ding calls it), given that she was days away from her official launch into Manila society as a concert pianist, and that she was by no means an official part of Zipper's orchestra. She was merely a stand-in for their pianist who had gotten himself so embroiled in anti-Niponggo efforts that he now finds himself in the innermost dungeons of Fort Santiago itself. Despite his 'tomfoolery,' I do wish he is alive, as I am almost sure that he is kin with the Fernandezes who have been kind to Alice and Ding, and have understood what this war might mean to newlyweds. If we are realistic here, it is a bittersweet marriage because these are such poor times. It is a happy marriage to Ding's kin, but I have made it clear that I have swallowed most of my pride at the match—I had always believed Alice would marry better given her strong (precarious, on stilts) station in life. I had told her as much the night before her wedding—but Alice had only told me that Ding was her *amor de vida*, and that she would go to the world's very end for him. How could one argue with that?

It was a fortunate match to the rest of Manila society who had believed Ding would marry one of theirs. They could not have abided that, given Ding's humble origins. And so Linang, one of theirs, had gone on to marry a Lacson, also one of theirs.

At any rate, I remain hopeful that the piano has been unplayed because I have taken it as a sign of Alice's general well-being. Alice made of music a kind of light in what she has often called the sad cathedral of her life—this 'sad cathedral' being something I have not entirely understood, and not entirely forgiven her for, given all the comforts she has enjoyed under my wing, and her father's money. Did any girl with her kind of privilege really look upon her life as a kind of ruin, a broken faith housed in the nave of a grand turret?

This always seemed to me to be the sentiments of an idle life—a life easiness and plenty had afforded her, and that our servants rubbed to a glad shine as they might every Sunday as they polished silverware. For Alice had learned none of the requirements of a lady: she had never learned how to cook or iron or mend. As far as I was concerned, any husband of hers had to content himself with knowing that any efforts she offered on any one or all of these fronts would be a beginner's efforts. That was almost unacceptable for me as a mother (or, if you will, a surrogate mother). For I had tried many times to teach Alice all these acceptable skills. She had spent her time instead reading books and learning the piano. She had also spent her time at the *Asociacion Feminista*, whose ladies declared that being a woman meant more than being a good wife. But what did they really know about that when I am almost entirely certain that all of those women knew how to mend and cook and iron, and I am one hundred per cent certain that these women married well—if not financially then politically?

I myself knew all these skills and had prided myself in knowing what few of those women knew: how to manage a business and how to survive a war and occupation with the fruits of this business. This was a skill I had hoped to be able to pass on to Alice, to little or no effect. So secure was Alice that there would always be food on the table three times a day, and that her clothes would be ironed and in place in her *aparador* a day before she needed them, and that there would be a feast on her birthday and every Christmas, as well as enough pocket money to indulge her every whim between holidays, that she could take to more gentle pursuits such as playing the piano. To my mind, the one misfortune of Alice's life was that she did not marry a rich man. Had she married well, my Alice would have thrived. I only wished that Ding would be as much credit to her as she is to Ding.

Understand that I do not mean to be unkind—it was only through my brother's efforts that I enjoyed the kind of standing I had in life. Ding had his own merits—didn't Ding bring honour to his country by being in the great Olympics of 1936? Hadn't he travelled in one summer more than Alice and I had ever travelled in our lives?

Still, we cannot help but hope highly and well for our children. To my mind, Alice should have married a man with means enough to indulge pursuits Alice had held close to her heart in her early adulthood. She should have married an *ilustrado* who could have shown her all the great cities of Europe, and taken her to see Debussy or Chopin or Beethoven played in their home countries, by their home orchestras, even centuries after their births and deaths. She would have done well to see first hand the cities of all the great painters and writers whose works she had seen only in books. But she didn't want any of these courting boys. She wanted Ding.

Ding, 1942

I have given up hope that the Americans will come any time soon, but I know that they will come.

These have been long and struggling days even as I have tried to keep them happy for Alice. The boys I know and have grown up with—even the scholarly boys I knew from school, most of them from better families than the boys I grew up with—have all joined secret movements, whether in Manila or in the Sierra Madre hills. They have joined what has been called the *guerillas without guns* movement here in Manila. Context clues remind me that there is such a thing as guerillas with guns, and that the best of our Berlin group may have gone up and joined them.

The more temperate boys from school have written for news sheets declaring Allied victories both big and small elsewhere in the world. They know that such news has brought courage and heart to a majority in Manila who have lost both, whether through personal loss or small everyday encounters with the Nips along our streets. Most of us who are married and either have children or are expecting children do not really care who wins the war as long as there is food on our tables for our women and children. To reach this larger, ambivalent demographic, the more cautious boys in my class went on to write propaganda newspapers that fell into the hands of many families like mine, and other families like Alice's. These papers spread far and wide across the city the way I imagine Rizal's novels had spread far and wide across Manila and its neighbouring provinces north, and south. Those, at least for me, were the real words, written in pages that were sure to indict their author, and did shortly thereafter. They were the real words because we fought an enemy within, and not some enemy brought here to lure a colonial power settled in these shores forty years ago. Then we were fighting a war centuries in the making—we were not allies to any world power: we were Filipinos fighting for our very freedom. We were not collateral damage, we were fighting for ourselves. This is what Alice has told me time and again because she does not have such a short memory as mine—her mind reaches years far ahead of ours, and they will continue to reach the years we will grow old in.

For now, war is the farthest thing from my mind—I do not think that I am less fearless than the boys in my class, I only think that I am more practical. I must do all that I can to ensure that my wife is fed and that my house is safe from any suspicion. I have learned the hard way what happens to regular Filipinos who are sympathetic to the American cause. Not too long ago, Alice's sympathies had landed a blow to my head and a heart-stopping spell at a *baluarte* named for a saint. Luck had saved me and Alice then, and I do not want to have to count on luck again. Alice and I are of one mind about this, as far as I can tell.

Our one married life is companionable and easy. We have learned to grow vegetables in our backyard and Alice and I have taken to eating fish with our rice. When there is no fish, we take to eating sweet potatoes and whatever cabbage will thrive in our backyard. We do not pay this any mind—we are prone to spells of laughter when we recall the old feasts in the dining halls of the old rich before the occupation. 'How the mighty have fallen,' Alice is prone to saying as she boils the sweet potatoes. 'At least we have sugar still, Ding, to dust over these potatoes. It would seem that we have saved our appetites for the very last part of a good meal—dessert.' 'Do you regret that most of our meals these days are desserts?' I have asked her. 'Darling,' she answers, 'all my teeth are sweet.'

Things are different, however, when her mother comes to visit. When she does—oftener these days than I'd like—she shakes her head at our lot. I know she holds me responsible for our meagre fare. She notes that there isn't meat in the house and then launches into the old impassioned Spanish how we are without shame. And by *we,* I know she means me.

Each time she does this, I feel a wild and sharp heaviness that could be tested into something more volatile if it weren't so quick to pass. Alice shoots me a sympathetic look when this happens, and wanly smiles.

One thing I know Salvacion is thankful for is how I've kept Alice safe thus far. If I am privy to the knowledge that boys like me have joined the resistance, she too notes that the ladies Alice grew up with have also joined the resistance—whether they are sending supplies to POWs in the old university or sending letters to guerillas in the hills. Alice has done nothing thus far to endanger our lives a second time, and seems far away from the days she was sympathetic to the American cause. When the official broadsheets had mentioned that there was a new symphony orchestra in town—the New Philippines Symphony Orchestra the Nips had orchestrated, Alice merely laughed. 'See what they have replaced the Manila Symphony Orchestra with, Ding?' A beat, and then: 'How laughable is this propaganda?

Now that is one orchestra I would never play for, even if they paid me in dollars,' she says. Then do I know that Alice has eased into our glad, quiet life. We are of one mind about survival during these dangerous times when members of prominent families we know—whether Filipino or mestizo—have been apprehended in their homes or bullied in their streets by the *kempeitai,* or even shoved and tortured in Fort Santiago.

I have wished only for the same kind of practicality as ours in these men and women. Like Salvacion, I do not know why they have been involved in such drastic movements. The Americans have come as they have always come. If I repeat this again and again, it is as much wish as it is faith. At least one of these things is sure to bring us an ending we can live with—I have always believed that all endings are happy ones. Should the present circumstance be anything less than happy, it is not yet an ending.

Besides, didn't we hear it from the lips of Douglas MacArthur himself that he will return? He has proven himself upstanding if not outright heroic. There is no doubt in my mind that before the war is over, he will have washed up on these shores, if only to fulfill the promise to end all promises. It is just a question of when. Not soon perhaps, but he will come. In the meantime, it is my main preoccupation in life to continue surviving and to keep Alice happy.

For the most part, I can tell you that she is. For she is happiest accomplishing the small tasks. She is happy when she has mended my shirts easily and ironed the collars with nary a crease in them, and ever so crisply. She is happy because she has never imagined she could manage such small expectations as dinner on the table and clean clothes, and being able to mend small rents in the fabric. She is happy because marriage has brought out her domestic side and has kept her fingers busy and nimble. And she is most happy when she is able to procure sugar and potatoes from the neighbour in exchange for a book or a glad hour playing the piano in their old house. 'See, Ding, despite mama's judgements about the finer things in life, they have proven useful during the war.'

We have grown so accustomed to our simple food that when Salvacion brings meat and chicken to the house, Alice's first thought is to give the food away to neighbours who are suffering 'infinitely worse' than we are. She has taken to bringing some of this meat—to my secret frustration—to the two spinsters up the street. Meat is so very hard to come by these days that even their simplest iterations on our table—*tinola* and not *relleno*, minced beef with *ampalaya* instead of a *mechado*—have been much-welcomed feasts. But I remember that it is Alice I have married, impractical and singularly beautiful Alice. Once again, I am happy for the sweet potatoes.

Salvacion, 1942

I remain afraid that Alice's present happiness hangs by a single thread, and that she will return any day now to her old ways. I see more and more signs in these recent visits. She is jittery and nervous. She is overly attentive. There is an unsettling, needy grip to her affection, as she kisses both my cheeks in greeting, draws me close in a tight hug. Alice knows I do not appreciate such overt displays, but she forgets herself. Sure, I have held her close—but with the kind of stiffness that proper decorum dictates. Understand that Alice was born during a hard season—it was the season of a great and deadly epidemic. When her biological mother had given us Alice in the San Lazaro hospital, the entire place had been in quarantine. Having come from such a place, our house on Cabildo Street had been marked against visitors and strangers with a red flag. This had meant that they were to keep away from my parents' home. That flag had been like lepers' bells to the outside world, but there inside the house were only my parents and myself and the beautiful child we had unexpectedly been called to bring into our world, for no other reason than that her father was ours.

Apart from her bad nerves, I have also seen sheet music on the piano and that it is Debussy, which only means that Alice is playing the composer she loves best. Someone not happy like Mozart, and not melancholy like Chopin, she is always liable to say. Someone perennially in between happiness and sadness, which perfectly describes not just the composer but Alice herself.

But these names mean nothing to me—I care as much for Mozart as I do for Chopin or Debussy, which is to say very little or not at all. These names are like English to me: they are foreign, newly acquired, and have not settled into my skin, or mind, or heart. Music is a language I scarcely know, and like English, it is a language I have only learned secondhand.

But these are telling signs, and I have always needed telling signs to understand Alice. I am not what you would call subtle or elegant. What is, is; what was, was. Black is black and white is white. This is not so for Alice who has always seen the world and life as an often-indeterminate gray. And even in that gray, there are nuances and variations. Charcoal. Ash. Wistfulness. Nothingness cast afloat by its own nothingness.

It is during these moments that I appreciate Ding for seeing the world as clearly as I do, and for knowing as I do, that all that is being required of us is to survive.

But back to Alice. Things alarmed me even further when, during my last visit, Alice had mentioned that she was now acting in plays with her friends Helena and Pilar. Both, I know are members of the Volunteer Service and Aid Committee—a group of women known for their feeding programs for orphans and abandoned wives (a group, I might add, almost descended immediately from the Asociacion Feminista, seeing as they are daughters of feminist mothers).

Aid for widows and orphans is, at least, is the official mission statement of the committee. Privately, I know that the girls are up to something more than civic duty. I know that Pilar has been known to exploit her beauty and charm to bring food and supplies to the prisoners of war in the old university. These deeds kiss danger, and do not bode well for Alice who has a rebellious streak in her and who is still so impressionable that danger might meet her mouth right back. If she does as she is told, she will land herself once more in Fort Santiago, and with less luck, perhaps, than she had the first time.

I think of what would calm down this wild nerve; I think long and hard about what will assuage this old and new wildness of feeling. I tell myself, 'Salvacion, you will know what to do, for you always know what to do.' And then the answer comes to me.

On my last visit, I tell Ding that he must give Alice a child.

If Ding has not been enough of a companion to keep her busy and fulfilled, then a child who requires all her attention and love will. At least, that is the hope.

Ding, 1942

Salvacion has pulled strings at the *Asociacion Feminista* and has procured from them a child from a widowed woman who has given up her child. I had not known this until the old woman had brought the child to our largely peaceful home, and our largely peaceful existence. I'll admit that I held this against her at first—the first reason being that she had noted that we had failed to produce by natural methods our own child, and that she took it upon herself to acquire one without our prior knowledge or approval.

But when she brings the child to our home in the form of small person of X, I see the rare joy in Alice's eyes. The child could pass as her own, if not mine. He is the yellowish kind of fair our own child would have been, given the darker shade of my skin and Alice's decided whiteness.

But his features are sharp, his jaw prominent, his eyes brown—and these are all Alice. When I see her face light up, I see that I have no recourse but to allow her to keep him.

It is almost immediately clear that the child has been broken—he clings so steadfastly to his teddy and sucks so fervently on his thumb that I quickly acknowledge that he will require some work. Within five minutes of his deposit—Salvacion calls him a gift, as though he were a trinket meant to tease Alice's happiness out of its steady hiding these days—I notice that the boy doesn't speak. 'Oh, can't we keep him, Ding?' she asks me. 'Of course we shall,' I tell Alice.

'What is his name?' I ask Salvacion. 'No name,' she answers, though I know this can't be true. A boy like this, even while abandoned, can't not have been named by its mother; can't not have been baptized in any one of the churches close by. But Alice only answers: 'How unfortunate for the poor dear. How very, very unfortunate.'

Salvacion purrs: 'But then you can name him, my dear. You can look at him, and spend time with him, and decide on a proper name.' A beat, and then an addendum. 'But make it Christian.'

Alice peruses the boy and opens her arms to him. 'Come,' she says. And the little boy runs to her arms, and I am sure then that she is his, as much as he is hers. I feel a momentary lightning on my chest, a sharp flash: this is almost the look she had first given me in love, but it is longer and softer.

She looks at the boy in the rags, clutching his soft teddy—no doubt a discard from a rich household, an old toy outgrown by the child of a wealthy family. I feel my heart mellowing slowly, beat by beat. 'What shall we name him, Alice?'

'Oh,' she says. 'We shall name him Bayani, for he has fought for his life during this whole occupation, and he has lost both father and mother besides, and still he has managed to survive.'

I know she sees herself in him—now they are twin orphans who have found each other.

Perhaps, it is the right name. Perhaps Alice is right. Perhaps, he is a hero.

Part Five

Manila, 1943-1944

Pilar, 1943

When the Manila Metropolitan Theatre opened a little over a decade ago, I took it to mean another marvellous act by new *ilustrados* to subtly and elegantly flout the efforts of the current occupation.

Our architects were also politicians, building American buildings but studying the latest European styles that would insinuate itself in our cultural centres. They were like certain politicians in high places who spoke of nationhood to the masses but then drafted pro-American bills meant to favor only American interests.

We had lived for decades marveling at the fruits of Burnham's City Beautiful movement—a vision of the old city that sang and stood with a staunch American imperialism. We saw this in their pillars and parks and spectacular views that inched ever so opulently and seamlessly into its crowning glory: Manila Bay. The city sparkled with a stunning visual symmetry—government buildings were linked with major thoroughfares. When grandeur threatened to turn into large-scale pomp, public parks eased the eye with wide spaces and lush trees.

Manila became a modern city, a rational city, a city made from a blueprint. It was this blueprint that turned the Philippines decidedly and systematically into an imperial democracy. It irked me to know that this new version of Manila had gained fame as the so-called 'pearl of the orient.' At best, it is an insipid slogan; at worst, it is the Americans patting themselves on the back for a job well done.

When the MET opened in 1931, here finally was a building I could marvel at. Here finally was Europe and not America. Here too was Asia. Gone were the neoclassical structures. Here, we found Cambodian temples in local minarets; we found stained glass panels by Kraut Grass—and yet we also returned to our roots with iron gates festooned with oriental flora and fauna. And then we ventured east with Hindi sculptures fixed to stunning parapets, fire and fern fronting the spectacular edifice.

Surprisingly, astoundingly, here too was Paris. Those of us who had always dreamed of travelling to the city of light need not have dreamed any longer, for Paris had come to us. It had come to us through the methodical madness and grandeur of the Art Deco movement.

It was here that I realized that its architects and artisans— Arellano and Tampinco first among them—that our artists and craftsmen had finally rebelled against our widespread colonial affectations. This was no longer Arellano's Post Office in Manila, this was Arellano's mad masterpiece. If we couldn't assert our independence by force, we could assert it through magnificent acts of small cultural rebellions.

Outwardly, the MET had been both rebel act and complete colonial history. Inwardly, the movies I had watched within it had local reverberations. I remember seeing *The Last Days of Pompeii* within its walls as a child. 'The Last Days of Manila,' my father had called it, seeing as how so many of his friends had turned into pro-American politicos if only to survive. I know he had seen them in the blacksmith-turned-gladiator. Meanwhile, I had seen the Philippines in the gladiator's son who had found Jesus. Nowhere there had I seen the common Filipino or the modern Philippines, except in Arellano's jut in the chin—for that was what the MET was, at least symbolically. We didn't know then that the last days of Manila already loomed across the horizon, and that it would only be a matter of time before Manila as we knew it would be no more.

Devastation came in the Japanese attacks of 1941, and here we find ourselves presently, taken by force into yet another occupation. My own heart has been addled by so much defeat, nothing lifts it. I do not believe that the future will be rosy, but I do believe that whatever its outcome, I am young enough to surmount it.

First, they came for us, revving their one-cylinder motorcycles in our major boulevards. They did not come as terrorists, they came as orderly as our Sunday tables and niceties. But unlike our Sunday tables, they also came noisily, burning rubber throughout the silent city.

During the night, they terrorized us with sundry blackouts. Often, there were also bombings that shook us out of our very skin, our nerves as fizzled and frayed as the cables lining our streets. The so-called pearl of the orient had been crushed into a fine powder, if not hurtled out to sea and left to sink into its silent wash and ebb.

Our elders thought that that was the end of us, but I knew better.

A year into the occupation, we had grown used to watching their movements. We knew that with wile and charm enough, we would find a way to survive and lend a hand to those who needed it most. At first, war widows and orphans; later on, we had settled on more daring acts of resistance. We had taken to bringing food to POWS from Bataan and Corregidor who were detained at the old university. We did this with secret messages hidden in the false bottoms of bags that carried letters and supplies to American sweethearts in UST, or Filipino sweethearts in the Sierra Madre Hills.

To obfuscate our movements, my friend Helena had formed a graciously benign group called the Volunteer Social Aid Committee. Publicly, we oversaw feeding programs for orphans and widows. Privately, I suppose you could call us (alternately) proud Filipinas, or resistance Filipinas, whatever suits you best when you try to understand our aims and our activities during these brutal days. Yes we fed casualties of the Japanese attack, but we also passed on intelligence gathered from various sources—sometimes it was from drunken *kempeitai* in places like Club Tsubaki who robbed us and used our women. Others from our own ranks monitored Japanese movements coming from imperial barges at the bay. This information we passed on to the more active women of the resistance—if we were intelligence officers, they were guerillas; settled into the hills above Laguna de Bay. They would pass this intelligence to their men and their men would pass this intelligence to American guerillas with shortwave radios who sent messages to MacArthur. First in his Australian headquarters and then to his New Zealand one.

Japanese brutality did not faze us—it made us gnash our teeth in anger, and it strengthened our resolve.

Pilar, 1944

It's come to my attention that I have a friend who has recently acquired—through wit and wile—a Japanese radio station. She has been propositioned by a businessman she calls only 'Taki' to promote Japanese propaganda. This comes largely in the form of Japanese music and news programs, but my friend—let us call her Y—has used these programs to promote another kind of propaganda altogether. The method is simple: Taki gives her a script to follow to promote their cause, but Y improvises on these scripts with messages to the resistance. She hides these messages in English so obscure, they are almost poems. Through these messages, she offers advice to common Filipinos on how to survive life under the Japanese. Some days, when the Japanese move dangerously into the hills, she passes military intelligence to guerillas.

I know that ordinary citizens fear for their sons in the hills and for their women in the streets. I know further that some of them haven't seen their sons in months, if not short years, and have no way to communicate with them. This is especially heartbreaking for me because these are the very boys I grew up with—their parents the *kumpadres* and *kumadres* of my own mother and father.

Keeping these boys alive could be as simple as giving their mothers and fathers aloft with the hope that they are alive. Hope has so often awakened into survival. If they didn't care about their lives, they would be needled and cajoled by hope to care about preserving their children.

Often *kempeitai* suspecting their sons of guerilla activity have fixed themselves outside these Manila homes, waiting for their sons to come home. One hears stories of unfortunate and ill-timed homecomings that have ended with arrests and certain death in Fort Santiago. That I almost understand. What I do not understand is how my father's old *kumpadres* have also been arrested and tortured in the old fort as well, even if they carry no information about their sons' whereabouts, and haven't seen them in years. I know I must find a way to keep these boys forewarned against the *kempeitai*. I know I must do it through methods as obscure as Y's 'poems.' And so, I approach the only artist among us.

I approach Alice Feria. I approach her for a plan to reach our boys in the hills. I approach her to remind her of the secret plots she has learned from books to write them into a believable plot. I tell her we need to save our boys.

Y, 1944

Pilar has come to me with a cause that isn't quite as close to my heart as leading a Japanese army into a mountain foothold and having my men in the bushes, waiting for a proper ambush. I have not given much thought to young men within my ranks who hanker to see their parents and sweethearts back home. Karma can't be on their side. For just as they have ambushed unwitting Japanese soldiers in the hills they do not know, so too have they been ambushed in front of their homes by *kempeitai* officers they do not know.

Pilar has told me that she and a young socialite and writer have found a way to send a message to these boys. They will stage a play, Pilar says—a European play at the MET itself. I ask Pilar how exactly this play will help send messages to our boys in the hills. She says that it will be a play about letters, specifically about a French soldier and rogue named *Cyrano de Bergerac.* It is an obscure reference, even for me. I know the plot: rogue Cyrano loves his cousin Roxanne who is as beautiful and cultured as he is ill-made and freakishly-nosed. Cyrano knows how to make mad music with words—so sharp is his wit and so red is his ardour for his cousin. Alas, Roxanne doesn't love Cyrano. She loves, instead, the handsome Christian whose youth and beauty cannot compensate for his shyness and embarrassing lack of profundity. Cyrano then pens the letters for Christian and acts as both writer and messenger, bringing to Roxanne Christian's ardour in Cyrano's pen.

I shake my head at Pilar when she brings me the stunt. She explains, 'Alice and I are sending messages to the people in the audience that they can send letters to their boys through the VSAC, specifically through us. Letters in code to warn their boys whether or not it is safe to come home.' I nod my assent even if I do not trust the plot.

Y, 1944

As promised, I have at great risk invited Alice Feria to the news program. She has relayed over the microphone exactly what Pilar has promised. She says that she and her fellow committee members are staging Cyrano de Bergerac at the MET. She further obscures the message by saying that the play will be staged in a new Tagalog translation—I understand immediately that this will be done so that the language will be lost to the Japanese in the audience. 'Tagalog,' she announces with the clipped cadences of the upper class, 'has been used consistently as a medium, and hence this language also helps to bring drama to the people.'

I smile at her but shake my head at the far-fetched ruse. 'The country's playwrights should go ahead writing plays, bearing in mind that they have a great cultural responsibility toward molding the country's culture through the stage.'

She talks briefly about nation-building and nationalization, and then continues: 'The theatre, as well as universities should be institutions in which the purity of our Tagalog is filtered, and from which theatre-goers could absorb consciously and unconsciously its substance and beauty. A well-organized theatre does not only dignify the nation's language but also gives breath to all walks of life as it is the synthesis to all the arts,' she says, giving me a polite smile.

On-air, I thank her. Off air, she draws me to a hold that catches me quite off-guard. 'Thank you,' she says 'for all that you've done, and for all that you are doing.' And then she turns and leaves me to talk of *The New Philippines Orchestra*, that will be playing in a few days, also at the MET.

To obscure Alice's message further, I tell our listeners of the repertoire, because I know that the Japanese are listening in. 'The orchestra will feature an overture by our very own Liwanag Cruz, Taga-Bundok, I say, as a further nod to our boys in the hills. And for our friends who we have gladly and whole-heartedly welcomed to these shores, the orchestra will also play Kosak Yamada's *Meiji Syooka*, that's Hymns to the Meiji Period to you and me. And with this, I happily and gratefully sign off, good night, and thank you to everyone who is listening in tonight.'

Pilar, 1944

The citizens among us have understood the message and have come proffering letters and dried fish and vegetables and rice in loot bags to our next VSAC meeting a day after the Tagalog translation of the Rostand classic is staged at the MET. In the absence of male players, all of us in the committee had had to play all the roles—me as Roxanne, Helena as Cyrano, and Alice as Christian. The rest as various villains and minor characters.

Y warned me that the play had roused Taki's suspicion and that he had shown her his badge as a subject of the imperial court. He had done this to warn her against any further high jinks, if that was what this play was, and that he would not spare her life or the lives of any of her friends should events play out and reveal themselves as plots against the occupation. The very day Taki had warned Y, we found a *kempetai* Officer at the MET, after we had dispatched the day's batch of goods and letters.

Alice and I were arrested for what the officer called 'disturbing the peace.' This did not land us in Fort Santiago, as I had originally feared. This had landed us instead in a local precinct where we were interrogated and kept.

I slept badly on Alice's lap, and she kept awake all night, worried about her husband and child. It was dawn when I woke and saw Alice pacing to and fro the left of the cell and the right. 'You must sleep, Alice,' I told her. 'How can I, Pilar? Ding must be worried sick about me, and he must be concocting all sorts of white lies for Bayani who is too young to understand any of this.'

By some strange supernatural luck and around noon, an officer had turned his key in the lock and announced to us that we were free to go. We did not know what or who had won us our freedom—our deed did not even merit an interrogation. When we left the precinct, we saw our answer. Standing not two feet outside our door was an elderly gentleman who announced himself not to me but to Alice. 'Alice Feria?' he asked. 'Yes,' Alice said tentatively. 'I am your Uncle Francisco's friend. We met several years ago in your grandparents' house on Cabildo Street.' He introduced himself as one Mr Roxas, a municipal judge. His ties to Alice suddenly seemed clear. They were legal ones, career ones, with her lawyer-uncle. But Roxas did not smile in familiarity. His eyes were cold, and his manner terse.

'I told your uncle that I will do this for you once, and once only,' he said. 'I am risking too much by even being here. The lives of so many are at stake just by my presence here,' he said sternly, archaically. 'This is not a game for you young girls to play. You are playing with your lives.' It took me a nanosecond to quote to him a writer I admired. 'If not our lives, then what else is there to play with?' I asked him, with the kind of brazenness that always landed me in trouble.

The old man shook his head and sighed. Neither Alice nor I merited a paternal kiss. The old man did not even shake our hands.

Barely a year later, I learned that the old man Roxas had harbored guerillas in his Manila home, and that once more he would harbour into his stern auspices the lawyer Feria, and his sister Salvacion, and their shared ward Alice.

Part Six

1945

One

The officer has just asked Alice and her husband Ding to gather all the drapes and rags in her house. He resembles the kenpei who had wrested her from her home and dragged her to Fort Santiago three years ago. She remembers briefly the piano, the dungeon, and then Haruki who she has not seen since the day he rescued her: his eyes scouring the bars, his finger pointing at her, the dungeon master opening the cell, and then Haruki bounding up the steps and disappearing into the old city. Haruki, the gentle father of roses. There was not one rose he did not know how to make live. She does not know why she remembers this now when this kenpei has singled out her house, her husband, her child.

She is sure now that this is indeed the officer who had arrested her some years before. He smells to her like tobacco and whisky and piss. She sees that he has climbed the ranks now: he brandishes a gun and not a bamboo sword.

He had wanted to watch her die three years ago, and now she thinks that he is her angel of death. Failing then, here he is again now, in her Malate home, asking her to gather her drapes and clothes, and kitchen rags, and potholders, and towels. 'Bring,' he only says, in an English she strains to understand, 'bring.' 'Mama,' her son, Bayani says, 'Mama.' Because he doesn't continue, she knows her son is scared witless and white.

Alice brings Ding's one good suit—the pinstriped one, the one he married her in. Why she does this, she doesn't know. She thinks that if she is honest with her prizes—if she brings to Saigo not only her bad rags but her good clothes (and then not even just her good clothes, but also the diamond brooch her aunt Salvacion gave her on her wedding day, Saigo will spare them).

The brooch is a bright oval, moored in the centre with a large diamond. The gaudy stone flits out into elegant curlicues dotted with smaller diamonds, into shapes that resemble snowflakes. It is an Art Deco brooch, her Spanish-speaking aunt had said in English, pronouncing it *ahrt decco,* the memory of which makes Alice laugh despite herself. 'Why laugh?' Saigo asks, 'why laugh?' Alice shows him the brooch, says, *please.* Saigo only snatches up the oval trinket, and glances at the healthy mound of clothes and rags. He douses the pile with gasoline.

In the living room, where they are gathered, there is only one place to hide—an impractical place that cannot survive a fire, but can only make it thrive. It is Alice's practice piano, fire's lush friend, its accomplice and *compañero.* When Saigo leaves with his pack of underlings, the house is already on fire. The fumes make Alice sleep.

Two

When Alice awakens, Bayani's hand is already limp in hers; when Alice awakens, Ding is gone, the fumes having seeped too deeply into his charred lungs. Ding has always been delicate—he has been prone, all their married life, to the frequent cold given the slightest shift in weather.

I love you, I love you, she tells her husband and son. She will not know if they heard. She breathes deep into the fumes, breathes deep and long, because she means to die. *What is life,* she tells Ding, *without you. What is life,* she tells Bayani, *without you. Goodbye, I love you,* she tells them. Tells Ding in his *camisa de chino,* tells Bayani in his smart sailor's suit, worn today because he means to be a sailor, he had told his mother not eight hours before, he had meant to sail away.

When Billy Fernandez, the neighbour's boy, pulls her out of the burning house, he will have saved her life. She will hate him for it forever.

Three

Billy Fernandez, all of ten, and raised by his parents to be brave, has just drawn Alice Feria-Obordo out of a burning house. He does not know how he has been able to do it with the woman clawing at him and shouting shame into his face— specifically, how he is without it. She is saying *verguenza*, or yet, more specifically, *sin verguenza*. Alice, the toast of their street, who has never been without a compassionate word. Once, he had brought Alice to the home of Felicidad and Corazon, two homely spinsters who lived in a grand old house down the street. Felicidad and Corazon had mostly been abandoned by their wealthy, older and married brother, Teodoro—who, for a small token fee each month, and paid to him, bought the right to stay in their childhood home. The two lived mostly on the Christian kindness of their neighbours.

Billy had carried, for a good block and a half, Alice's market basket to the spinster's house. There was a fresh roast inside, and vegetables enough to last a week. The house smelled like lavender and mothballs. When their bell rang, Billy had heard

Corazon pronounce urgently to her sister that it was Teodoro, their eldest brother, come to collect the rent. 'Tell him we are busy with lunch, tell him to come back tomorrow.' Billy knew there wasn't any lunch to be had. He had heard, instead, the hiss of a shirt pressed urgently against a wet pan. It was the sound of meat cooking. It was the smell of nothing. Felicidad had opened the front door to a crack the width of an arm. 'Alice!' She had said, 'And Billy!' She had squeezed her left hand through the gap in the door and pinched his cheek. 'I'm sorry we can't let you in—sister is cooking lunch!' 'Then you will have no use for this,' Alice had said, gesturing toward the basket hooked on both Billy's hands. Felicidad had looked hungrily at the roasted fowl covered in a sheet embroidered with a curlicued *AFO*. 'Corazon is busy with lunch, but please leave the basket for Teodoro who is stopping by just a little later.'

Billy remembers that no sooner had they stepped out into the street then Felicidad had unlatched the lock, grabbed the care package, and torn inside, proclaiming to her sister that Alice Feria-Obordo had proffered not just fish, but fowl, a full fowl basted in butter and garlic.

That Alice had been white and kind, her eyes looking down on Billy's young face. 'You must never tell anyone what we have just seen here,' she told Billy. 'You must promise, Billy.' 'I promise,' Billy had said, gazing into her brown eyes. She had ruffled his hair. 'One day, you will find a girl lucky enough to marry you,' Alice had told him. Billy then only wanted to marry Alice. *That* Alice.

This Alice is red and screaming and furious. Her entire, godly face has been bloated to the colour of a scrambling crab. And then, not just her face, but her arms. 'You are hurt, Mrs Alice,' he says, 'you are terribly, terribly hurt.'

Billy remembers his mother's admonitions: 'If we are ever to separate, Billy, if our house is ever to be shelled, we must meet, Billy, at Remedios Hospital.'

Remedios Hospital two blocks south of Calle Real, Calle Real which you could meet by turning left down his street. He knows he must take Alice to this hospital, which will be doubly hard to do because Alice is easily twice his weight. Thrice, now that she has fainted.

Four

Salvacion Feria does not know what to do. The gunfire and the bombing have finally stopped. She has no money except for Mickey Mouse money—currency printed by the Japanese after they sent the country's valuable reserves to Japan. Salvacion has hundreds of these bills, useless now after the liberation.

What isn't useless is the small *baul* she has hidden in her backyard. In the small chest, she has kept what she now knows is the world's one true currency: jewelry. In this small *baul* is a ten-carat diamond, two tortoiseshell hair combs and a diamond brooch. It is the twin brooch to the one she gave Alice on her wedding day. She gathers her gray hair into a chignon. Within that large, peppered lump, she has hidden the diamond. She has held it in place with the tortoiseshell combs. The necklace and earrings she has hidden in a silk scarf she has marred, deliberately, with wet mud. They kiss the chignon when she wraps the scarf under her chin.

She has found, through all her crazy meandering in Manila's rubbled streets, Malate. She has coursed through Calle Real.

She knows this is Alice's Street, but she cannot find Alice's house. For sure, Alice must be dead, she thinks and weeps. 'Poor Alicia,' she weeps, 'poor Alicia.' Now, no longer a mother, she allows herself grief. She is prostrate and on her knees when the kind Fernandezes find her, and coax her gently into her home. It has miraculously survived. Salvacion thinks, *how.* Despite her grief, she thinks, *how.* She looks at the door, at the small square of Japanese flag glued above it. Alice's neighbours have befriended, for all their traditional church-going, traditional Filipino-ness, the enemy.

Unsurprisingly, she admires their gumption, their instinct to survive. Unsurprisingly, she chuckles despite herself. When she enters their home, there is Billy playing under the *carroza*. Home, to many Octobers, to our *Lady of La Naval.* 'Billy,' his mother Wilhelmina says, 'this is Lola Salvacion.' Billy pays the old woman no mind—she looks to be ancient, at least fifty years old, just like his *abuelita.* 'Billy,' her mother starts again. 'Lola Salvacion is the mother of our neighbour, Alice.' Billy at last, looks up. 'Please say your condolences. Lola Salvacion has just lost Alice.' 'No, she hasn't,' the boy says. Salvacion pulls him from under the carroza, '*Que?*' she asks. '*Que?*' Billy tells her that two days before, he had drawn Alice out of her burning house. It is a knowledge not even his mother is privy to. 'What do you mean, Billy?' his mother asks. Amid the confusion, the boy is silent. 'What do you mean, Billy?' she asks again, sharply this time. The boy tells her that Mister Ding is dead, that the boy, Bayani, is dead, but that Alice is very much alive, and that he had taken her, not two days before, to Remedios hospital.

Five

Salvacion lets the boy lead her through the rubble and ash of Manila, through the razed sadness of Calle Real, to Remedios hospital. For his troubles, she gives the boy the poorest of her treasures—this much she owes him for saving her daughter's life. She gives him the sapphire earrings—not a poor treasure, by any means, but a modest one relative to her bright diamond, the tortoiseshell combs, the brooch, and the emeralds. 'Keep this, Billy, for a rainy day, she says,' adding a nanosecond later, 'don't tell your mother.' Billy leaves her at the gate of Remedios hospital.

Salvacion wanders through endless hallways festooned with hospital cots, tended to by men much too young to be doctors—they remind her of her brother, Felix in that lost time, in a poor town in Bukidnon. She gazes at row upon row of burned casualties. She has seen women and men like these along Malate, watching movies at the Zen Cinema. She has seen their mothers praying at church, their fathers brushing elbows with Americans, hearing them call out, *How can I help you, sir,* from their establishments, their soda fountains, their *panciterias.*

She has spent an afternoon spying faces she knows, or faces she thinks she knows, but she hasn't spied Alice.

It has been a long day—to walk endless streets, to believe your daughter to be dead, and then to know she is alive—Salvacion wants nothing more than to rest on a hospital cot, with its rickety, barred headrests—but all the cots have been taken. She lays herself on the floor, beside a cot occupied by a boy not more than fifteen, crying out for his mother. *Sin verguenza,* she tells him, you are practically a man, what are you doing, crying for your mother?

Tomorrow, she will find Alice.

Six

A nurse has given Salvacion some rice, salt sprinkled on it because there are no viands to be had, no hard beef, no fish, even. Salvacion eats it greedily, with her fingers, the way her mother Dolores taught her, gathering the rice into stiff clumps with her fingers, pushing the rice into her mouth with her thumb. She needs all her strength. She tells the nurse she is looking for her daughter. The nurse knows it is a long shot. 'Many mothers have lost their daughters, Ma'am. Are you sure your daughter lives?' she asks Salvacion. Salvacion thwacks the hard dish on the floor. 'I know my daughter is alive, *ma'am.*' The last word she brandishes with sardonic exaggeration. This nurse is no *ma'am*, she is barely an adult. She sees the fear in the nurse's eyes, knows this shivering young thing could be her key to Alice. Salvacion mellows. 'I am looking for my daughter, Alice,' she explains. 'Alice Feria-Obordo. Perhaps you can lead me to her. She has just lost her husband and child. She is only a young wife,' she says in the Spanish the young nurse has learned from her parents. 'There is a young woman here,' the young nurse says. 'She has been calling out for her husband and young child.' Salvacion pulls herself up from the floor. 'Tell me where she is, tell me,' Salvacion snaps.' The young nurse winces, thinks of future pain in this woman's hands. This woman, old enough to be her lola, with her whiskered mole and un-Christian impatience.

The nurse leads Salvacion to a young woman not three beds away from their scuffle. Salvacion holds her breath. Light hair, pinched nose. Salvacion's heart stops. Salvacion *peruses:* the eyes, the nose, the rather plain beauty. Salvacion's heart starts again. This is not Alice. This is Alice's friend, Linang.

Seven

There is another girl, the nurse says, who fits the profile. Salvacion tells Linang all will be well, all will be well, but that she must draw now to the great anonymous the young nurse leads her to. This girl has her entire face bandaged up, her eyes drawn to the jagged lines of a bare squint. She is delirious. 'Mama!' the girl calls out, 'Papa!' Alice has never known her mama, has just glancingly known her papa. Still, in her delirious hope, Salvacion owns that this might be Alice in a fever dream. 'Alicia,' she says, '*si, si,*' the burned young woman replies. For days, Salvacion tends to her—lifts to her mouth the watered rice in a blunt fork, where the watery sludge slips between the tines; strokes the light brown hair that sticks limply to her neck. 'You must re-gain your strength, Alicia,' Salvacion says.

She prays, daily, a novena to Our Lady of Remedios, she has stated intentions: that Alice may recover, that Alice may accept losing Bayani, and Ding. On the fourth day of the novena, the nurse decides it is time to check if the young girl's wounds are healing right; that it is time to change her bandages. Salvacion, as her only guardian, willingly obliges.

As the young nurse uncoils the dry bandage, Salvacion once more holds her breath. The girl is plain, her nose the nose of the common *indio,* wide and brown. She moves to strike the young nurse who cries out at the top of her lungs, *lo siento*, I'm sorry, *lo siento.* Salvacion lifts her right hand to the girl's face, leaves a mark as red as raw beef, and starts to weep.

A few cots away, Alice Feria-Obordo is having a fever dream. She is marrying Ding Obordo. She is telling him to have and hold her life. He has, and he holds. And then, she watches as he burns.

Part Seven

Burt Winn, 1945

When Burton Winn walks into the Roxas ancestral home in Manila, his eyes sweeping past the length of the room, he gives a low whistle. Back where he is from, they don't have foyers filled with ancient Chinese vases with blue, oriental scribbles festooned on them to indicate 'double happiness;' they don't have wooden lounge chairs or porcelain tchotchkes behind the glass of expensive cabinets.

They have farms in Deerfield Massachusetts—they have apple orchards and cows he and his brother Francis were taught to milk when they were five and seven, respectively. Grip and slide, their daddy had said: grip the udder with your thumb and forefinger, and slide. Francis had always gripped too hard, but Burt had learned the trick almost immediately, had shrieked 'eureka' when milk first spluttered into the can—the handle askew and torn from a screw.

In Manila, Winn is in the house of a powerful Filipino clan, whose power extends to their contemporaries and colleagues in Philippine society. You could find in their living room people called Lacson, Guerrero, and Ledesma. You could find them enthralled when the young widow they called Ferry played a nocturne by Chopin on their Steinway.

Among themselves, the officers under Winn trade gossip about the widow's face—burned they say during the liberation in her Manila home, her face so blistered and red, that the soldiers have taken to calling her Crab Face. They have never done so in the presence of the Captain knowing that he would not approve.

Burt sees how her fingers glimmer across the piano during the sweeping flourish and familiar refrain of the piece. She does not look fully Filipino—she has light, hazel eyes and a thin nose.

You can tell from her eyes that she is absent from this scene. She is doing things by rote, by blind routine. 'Bravo,' calls out Mr Roxas. 'Again Alice, again!' Alice? Burt thinks. He guesses Ferry is a nickname, but how it's derived from such an elegant name as Alice, he can't guess.

He watches her from the doorway leading from the foyer to the living room. He leans against the frame for the entire duration of the piece. His spine is grooved on the wood as he leans on his right leg. The piece is so long, his back has started to hurt. As they applaud, Ferry smiles wanly and looks up. Her eyes meet Burt's—but what for him is the shock of recognition, what for him is a shared, ancient sadness, and what for him is one soul encountering another, is something completely different for her. Her eyes narrow when she sees the fair-haired American standing in the doorway of a grand home in Manila, a genteel abode that the Americans have turned into one of their makeshift headquarters. She is trying to smile, Burton thinks, but Alice Feria is not trying to smile. There is no tenderness to Alice Feria's gaze. She is not reeling from any kind of ancient sadness.

She is thinking that despite being reared in Christian goodness, despite being taught to love one's neighbour as one loves oneself, when she sees the American casually leaning on the doorway, the American who believes himself to be a hero—you can see it in the cockiness of his pose, in his magnanimous eyes that scour her own as if he knows her—Alice trembles. She has never been so angry with an American in her life.

Ay, Kalisud!

When the whole Roxas house is asleep, Alice is still awake. In the small hours, she has never been more herself. In the small hours, no one asks any questions. No one bothers with *How are you, Alicia?* No one recalls brief encounters with Ding (*He was the best of us, Alicia, I just want you to know*), or Bayani (*He was always such a good boy, Alicia, I just want you to know*).

No, in the small hours, Alice is allowed to grieve. There are no words to her grief in the English the Americans have made them learn, or in the Spanish she was raised speaking. Her grief is more ancient than that, more basic than that. She knows grief in her father's tongue, in Salvacion's tongue, in their native dialect. *Ay Kalisud.* Oh, how difficult. *Kalisud sang binayaan.* How difficult to be left. *Ay cielo azul, abaw diin ka na bala.* Blue sky, where are you? Help me, a prisoner of love. It is better to die, if by dying, I will not remember my unhappiness.

Now the gunfire and shelling have stopped to reveal pure, undiminished sky. How at odds, these blue heavens are, with the melancholy tune. In the small hours, Alicia does not check herself. *Ay Kalisud.* Soon the cook will rise, bothering herself with the day's rations. Soon, Master Roxas will rise, bothering the cook with the day's meals.

Alice looks out of the window of that borrowed room with Salvacion barely stirring on the bed they share. Alice looks out of the window in her blue nightgown, undone at the top button. The morning air is cool on her brisk skin. She is surprised she can still feel things as basic as air.

They tell her she is still here: the stupid sparrow trilling painfully on her ear. Soon, the blue sky, the first smells in the kitchen, boiling rice. The silly songs the American boys sing because they have made the Roxas house their own official playground.

These are innocent songs, romantic, courtly songs—and she will hear them, her blood hurting her temples, to remind her that she is still here. She is still here. How difficult. How very difficult.

Burt

The first time Burt Winn sees Alice Feria, she is looking out from the guest window of the Roxas house in Manila. It is six in the morning, not quite sunrise but the blue already lifting.

She had been singing a dirge-like song to no one in particular. He had heard this in the melody even if he hadn't understood the words. He hadn't seen her face as much as he had seen her form haloed in blue—a muted version of the kind of blue in religious Italian paintings, often in the hemline or veil of the Virgin Mary.

He has not been able to sleep since the liberation, walking around the Roxas grounds while everyone is asleep. He had thought he had dreamed her, the way he has dreamed other things—accidents often before they happen, a family death before the telegram arrives.

Sometimes people happen to him as colours first; sometimes there are scurrying shapes he does not want to see in the mirror.

It both fascinates and scares people when his eyes change colour: green at his birth, and green under even circumstances, during even days. His eyes turn grey when he is downcast or weary or carrying a terrible burden.

That afternoon, he had seen her in the Roxas sala playing the piano. Her face moon-shaped and white, her eyes light. He assesses her as being in her early twenties, her brow and mouth without any permanent lines of worry or age or hardship. He sees looseness in her dress, but they have all been through hunger and do not quite belong to their clothes. This time, he does not see that morning's blue softly shrouding her. He sees her hazel eyes, the thin arcs of her brows, her hair falling to just below her nape. Alice smiles at her hosts abstractedly. She is here but she isn't here, Burt thinks to himself.

These days he has begun to be friendly with the Roxas' and they include him in their casual talk, and in talk they do not let Salvacion or Alicia hear. When they speak to him of the widow Feria, and how she used to be beautiful before she had lost her family during the war and before the Japanese burned her house down—when they say between themselves, thank God for Billy Fernandez dragging her out of the burning house, but not before her face was ruined by fire—it's in such talk that he does not understand what they are saying, does not see what they see, thinks the war has played so much with their minds, their eyes must be broken.

Salvacion, 1945

When I rise, it is half past six in the morning and Alice knows that her private moments are over.

I scuttle over to the bedroom mirror fastened onto a stand. There is water in a basin and I wash my face. Only then do I notice that Alice's space on the bed is as pristine as she had left it the previous morning. The pillow unmussed, the mattress unlined. By habit, I look up at the *capiz* window, steps away from the bed. I see Alice looking out, blankly, into the morning. She is in one of her moods and so I hurry to her. 'Alicia,' I begin. 'Alicia, I know that you are hurting, but you are young yet. You'll learn, in time, that so much of your life has been unlived yet. That there are good things in store for you that you do not see yet.'

'*Si mamá*,' Alicia says. '*Si.*' I open an *aparador* with my last few treasures: a traje de mestiza with butterfly wings, now cinched at the waist as was the fashion of the time before the war. I button the top, and button the old skirt from behind. Half-starved during the war, and I still have my thick waist. I know I've missed one or two hooks given my middle-aged fingers, but it's no use to ask Alice for any kind of assistance. The girl is dumb with grief, with sleeplessness. I will let her sleep until noon.

I lead Alice to the bed and tell her to sleep. It is up to her now to keep up appearances. War-time, or not, this is not her house, and she must keep to its rhythms. She will wake when its masters wake, she will sit in the dining room, and be served whatever the day's rations are—sometimes it's rice with teaspoons of mangoes, sometimes it's rice with salted fish. Whatever the viand—meat or fruit—there will always be rice.

When I leave the room, the Americans are already carousing. They are singing songs from what I gather is an American *zarsuela* called Oklahoma. Two young officers singing about a silly morning in America. Their Captain, my favorite, is nowhere to be seen today. 'Oh! what a beautiful morning,' I hear them singing. 'Oh! what a beautiful day.'

When Alicia ambles into the living room, it is already half past noon. Mr and Mrs Roxas have already wondered how she is. They are elegantly placed on their long *mariposa*, eagerly awaiting Alicia's entertainments. Will it be Chopin or Mozart this afternoon?, they wonder aloud. I tell them, it will be whoever they want her to play. I give Alice a warning look. Alice shrugs.

It is a languid scene I know well—the well-heeled positioning themselves elegantly into the day, rapt with the idea of whatever entertainments await them. As guests here, our hosts ask to be entertained, and we pay them back with conversation and music, as though we were poor relations.

Never mind that I too have my own wealth hiding in the walls of their very bedrooms—a small trove that will tide us over after the war. This makes me smile, snidely, at the mistress' art deco earrings. The brisk, tiny diamonds set in what I know to be an illusion cut—not the five carats of their collective size.

Illusion like the peacetime that has levelled the old city into this ominous and devastated quiet.

Alicia, I have noted, irritably, is wearing the poorer of her cotton blouses. There are only two, but she has picked the coral one that does nothing for her. I would have preferred the blue one that complemented the cold tones of her skin. Especially now that the American Burt has positioned himself—more frequently these days—on the doorway of the grand living room, waiting to hear Alice play. Today, though, it isn't the captain leaning on the doorway, it is one of the gangly privates under him.

'I feel like a little Debussy today,' Alice says coolly to the Roxas couple. She ignores me and the American, and places her hands on their Steinway, playing by rote. As she plays the first phrase of music, the officer says, 'Oh that again. Can you play something more upbeat, something more modern?' he says with an eastern American draw (not drawl, that would sound easy on the ear, but *draw*, a libel on the lips, the way he says *mawdahn,* for modern).

Alice winces. 'And what would you have me play, today?' she asks the American. His eyes light up. 'Do you know "Oh What a beautiful morning?" Alice sighs to herself. 'No I don't. Perhaps señor will sing it and I will follow on the piano.' 'Gladly,' says the American. 'Señor will gladly sing it, and if you could oblige me, maybe you could play along.' Alice shrugs. 'Oh what a beautiful morning,' the American croaks. 'Oh what a beautiful day…--' The Roxas' clap. Alice sees me clasp my hands, shakes her head briskly. I know from her expression that his voice is terrible but she is doing nothing to hide or embellish his tone with music.

The chords are easy enough to learn. She follows that awful baritone with her fingers. 'I've got a wonderful feeling, everything's going my way,' he sings, encouraged by her playing. The song continues for a good two minutes—at the end of which, the American bows exaggeratedly to his Filipino audience, and they clap. *'Que maravelloso,'* I say, standing up from the loveseat where she has positioned herself beside Mrs Roxas. And then again, *'maravelloso.'* 'She means marvellous, officer,' says Mr Roxas, encouragingly. 'Simply marvellous.' 'Well now, I aim to please,' the American private says.

Alice rolls her eyes at the piano. *Marvellous for a frog,* she thinks to herself. The officer catches the young widow rolling her eyes. 'What's that now?,' he asks, used to being a white man in a colonial room. 'It's marvellous, Señor,' Alice says sarcastically. 'Simply marvellous.' 'Well now, I thought you would say that,' he whispers in her ear. Alice leans away from the odious American and wrinkles her nose. 'I thought you would say that, crab face,' he says.

Alice rises, angrily, from the piano chair. 'I beg your pardon, American,' she says, in disgust. I draw a horrified breath. 'But did you just call me crab face?' The American laughs. 'Yes,' he says breezily. 'Cause you're red as a crab now, aren't you? An angry red-faced crab.'

The Roxas' are hard to ruffle, but they look aghast. I think maybe it was wrong to call on old favors and take Alicia here. 'Alicia…,' I say. The young woman slams the expensive hood of the old piano, doesn't care she is a guest, points an angry finger at the young man. There is a riposte there but she cannot find the words for it. She only knows her anger, which blooms like blood in water. 'You,' she only tells the young man, flicking his nose with her long, white finger this time. 'You—' she says, as she exits gracelessly out of the room. She hears the young man's amused laugh. 'Why, señor would you call her a crab?' Roxas asked. 'That is hurtful. And the young woman has been through so much.' Even I have taken back to my seat, folding the hands that only seconds earlier had lauded the young man.

I follow Alice as she rushes angrily to the room we share. *Sin Verguenza, sin verguenza,* I tell her. I often told her this is as a child, when she crossed me with various childhood offenses or fell asleep during rosary. I often told her this when her young travesties lengthened into small sins. But this time, it isn't Alice who is without shame.

Guest in this household or not, I mean to speak my mind to the American when Alice has calmed down. I quite mean to fly into a rage. I know that Alice is thinking that the man himself is without shame—that she is using on him the words I've used on her so often in the past.

She is using them to describe to herself that laughing American. Only when we are both safely inside the room does Alice gather herself. Crab Face, the American had called her. She does not know what he means, until she does.

She has not looked properly into a mirror since I had rescued her from the Remedios hospital. I use the term 'rescue' loosely because I believe that she would have gladly lived out her days in that hospital bed, on nothing but gruel twice a day. That hospital would have been her own salvation.

She knows only that she has been badly burned, that her face had felt angry with fire when the boy Billy had dragged her out of her house. She remembers only that she had come to—who knows how long after—to find her face lined with bandages and sticking tape. She remembers my gasp when the nurse had unwound the long swathes. When she had asked me what the matter was, I had only uttered, archaically, gently, 'They are new wounds yet, they will heal.'

Alice knows it is the time for the inevitable. With a long sigh, she stands from the bed and clears her throat, squares her shoulders, the way a person might who is incredibly afraid, and who must now draw up some form of courage from a deep, unknown source.

Alice makes her way to the standing mirror, tilts her head to the right, draws it slowly to the centre. And there she sees what has made the American say it. *Crab Face*. It is a face bloated and red at the jaw. She knows now that these are wounds that will never heal by themselves. In between, patches of face as red as her jaw. 'Oh,' Alice only says. 'Oh.' She looks at me from where I'm sitting on the bed. 'Alicia,' I say. 'Oh.' Alicia says a third time, recoiling from her stranger's face in the mirror. 'Alicia,' I repeat. 'You never told me,' she says to me. 'You never, ever told me.'

I draw her to the bed, tell her, 'after the this is over, Alicia, I will take you to the best doctors. I will give them everything I have to heal you. Everything, Alicia. You have to believe me.' Despite herself, Alice allows me to fold her into my embrace. Her body shudders and my daughter keens.

Listening neighbours would have thought this was the death wail that accompanied mothers and widows when they heard of their own boys lost to the war. But it is not her husband and her boy that Alice is crying for. She is crying—for the first time in a long while—for herself. It is her face she sees, and yet not her face, that makes Alice gasp for air, tire herself out crying, then wailing, until the day is not a day, it is only one long endless grief.

* * *

In the dream he sees his mother in the kitchen table with her head bowed, tears done for the time being. She sits opposite Francis but their father isn't there with them. He thinks perhaps it is his father who has died.

'With him gone, Francis, I'd like to beg a question—does love exist even after death. I must assume it does. He said so himself,—he'd either been drunk or inspired by the spirit, doesn't matter which, but his eyes had danced in the kitchen light. He had said to me, "Perhaps all love in the end, all no-capitalized love, all small love blends into the one love, in heaven. Perhaps there all our small, imperfect loves will at last be fully realized".'

His mother wipes away her tears, and then Francis holds her for small seconds, as though he cannot bear his own grief and then his mother's all at once. And then he scurries away from the kitchen. As though Francis is still there, his mother continues. In the dream, he can see clearly the age spots on her hands. Her craggy forehead, her gold hair graying at the roots.

'He needn't have bothered me with talk of heaven to realize what he called a perfect love; my love for him was a perfect love—it was an earthly love, to be sure, but it was a perfect love. I knew every one of his yearnings and moods. More than I knew anyone, or he knew anyone, I knew him, and he knew me.'

He watches as his mother pours herself a brandy. At this point in the dream, she does not speak but he can hear her thoughts. In the dream, his mother calls him her testimony and her witness, and then he wakes. He realizes that it was not his father who died in the dream. It was himself.

He remembers how he had always listened to his mother's talk when his father was in his fields and Francis got caught up with girls. Burt remembers his mother telling him that her girlhood dream was to join the circus and to travel the world— he had listened to what his mother had thought was a small inconsequential story of her maiden days. Three weeks later, he had brought her back an old black and white photo from a Barnum and Bailey catalogue.

It was the picture of a girl on a tightrope. He was only a boy then—maybe eight or nine, and so he couldn't understand why the picture had brought his mother to tears. She had never felt so seen in her life. 'There, there, mama,' he had said. 'There, there—do you want me to take the picture back so you won't be so sad anymore, mama?' She explained that no picture could have ever made her happier. That he was her one true joy, that he was her circus wish and all her thousand imagined joys, fully realized.

Burt Winn Writes A Letter Home

Dear Mama:

There is a walkway by Manila bay where a bright orange sun dips down into the horizon at six in the evening. You don't see that kind of red, even in the kind of paradise I like to think of as home. The farther away I am from it, the more of a paradise it seems.

But what a place this was without this war, mama—government buildings with pillars and balconies, opening to wide, open spaces. And my life now seems just like that—a large reach into an unknown that seems less fearful now than it did just a few days before. I feel my life opening in a thousand new ways. As if at the end of a dark thoroughfare, the road had emptied into a lush garden.

Alice is from a good Manila family. She has been educated as a journalist and as a musician. She is comely and polite, her eyes with a touch of hazel in them—I have never turned an eye from beauty and so I gaze each day into its face.

Your loving son,
Burt.

There, he says to himself, sealing the envelope bound for a small town in Massachusetts. His first sense of Alice as a colour had turned now into a feeling. She made him feel the way he did in his father's apple orchards as a boy—the way he and Francis used to rub to a shine the speckled skin of apples with a little spit in a handkerchief. That red. That variety of red. That mottled sort of perfection.

* * *

In the dream Burt arrives at the depot expecting Francis but seeing Sawyer, Francis' best friend. Sawyer waves his hands wildly as the train pulls into the station—his hair miscast, his face flushed. Even in the dream, it's a great blow to him to see his brother's substitute. He will not take the hand Burt holds out to him, looks disdainfully at Burt's instead. 'Hello Sawyer,' Burt says. 'Pity Francis couldn't be here.'

Sawyer ushers him into his father's car and says that Francis was held up at the farm, that an old cow had died birthing her colt and that his brother took it upon himself to nurse that baby back to health. More than the lie, it is a greater blow to smell moonshine on Sawyer's breath. Burt had naively thought that he was above day drinking. He smells like gin and shoeshine and he tells this to Sawyer.

Burt knows that Sawyer dodged the war pretending injury. Day of the draft, he'd had his younger brother Tom split his right shin with a B.B. gun. Next day, he'd had his mother contest his eligibility for the war. Burt has never had any respect for Sawyer, but has always had only the utmost respect for Francis.

But Francis sending Sawyer to the depot instead of meeting him in person himself—a brother he hasn't seen in close to five years—sends the clearest of signals.

In the dream, he is on his way home to tell his mother that his Filipino wife is with child. He knows these words will break her heart; he also knows that nothing in this world can stop him seeing her to tell her the news.

In the dream, Burt tells Sawyer that he first wants to see his father's orchards. He has not seen trees rife with apples in five years. He wants to scour his father's lands and bring to his mother the best and brightest apple.

For once, Sawyer complies simply and without hesitation. And then they are in the orchards, and Burt runs up and down their flush rows as gleefully as a child suddenly home from school or escaping his father's belt.

Burt appraises apples, thinking which one to best gift his mother. It takes him time to find the trees with the green ones. He knows she has always loved the tartness of the greens, and not the sweetness and fragrance of the reds.

In the dream, Burt finds the right one. It is flecked with white near the stem, but is a bright green everywhere else. It is the right apple to bring his mother as a 'conciliatory' gift, but even in the dream he knows he has nothing to be sorry about. He will only pretend it is a conciliatory gift. His mother will think he is sorry for his Filipino wife; and she will accept the false apology. It will be a kind of comedy of manners. Neither of them will mean anything they will pretend to mean.

In the dream, he wraps the apple in the bright, white kerchief Alice has embossed with a curlicued AFW in blue sewing. *Alicia Feria Winn.* It is the right gift. He knows it will tell his mother all the right things about her upbringing.

He and Sawyer have raced the entire lengths of this orchard to find this apple. He sees them whizz through the earth, melting back into their childhood limbs. He sees them laughing as they did as boys, and then he remembers how before Sawyer was Francis' friend, he was first his.

Salvacion

Since that afternoon, I do not see again the young officer who had called Alice Crab face.

The young captain, however, is here almost every day. He is attentive to her, escorts her from lunch to the living room where her hosts clap for Chopin or Rodgers and Hammerstein. He draws her chair for her before she sits at the piano. He claps loudest when she finishes a piece, asks her if she wants water, brandishes a handkerchief for her to wipe her brow after a ridiculously long encore.

When he notices that she is too tired to play, he yawns exaggeratedly, and tells the master of the house that it is too good a day for music, that it is a day for dreaming and siestas. Roxas almost always agrees, tells everyone else that at last the Americans have learned their customs and ways. He suggests a siesta and claps his hands. Burt gives her a wink and escorts her to the foot of the stairs.

He is more attuned to her than she is to herself. She does not know herself. She does not eat or sleep. She might chatter excitedly at lunch one second, and then bow her head before her plate as though she'd suddenly remembered something unspeakable but torrential. He knows that it is during these moments that she remembers her husband and child. Such dark silences fall on the table when this happens that Burt has learned to think on his toes, crack the right joke, praise the host for that or this.

Burt wants to see her as often as he can—he knows that if he is invited to lunch, he must earn his way to an invitation for supper. He does this by bringing rice or whisky from the black market for Roxas. When he can't bring both or either, he plucks roses from the neighbour's garden to bring to Mrs Roxas.

When Burt tells me that his older brother was raised to be a farmer, and to be first among his father's lands, as heir and master, I think Burt was born to be a hero, and that his mother must have known this from the time he was born. I think he must have been born fully-formed and handsome, unlike other babies I have seen who have been born scaly and thin and veined like lizards.

He told me that he knew he was his mother's favourite when, at five, he had winked at her when she charred a roast and he'd proclaimed it the unfoulest fowl he had ever tasted, the cheeriest and gladdest and tastiest chicken in all of Massachusetts. If he had been her secret darling before that day, he was her obvious love thereafter.

When the American shows not just a passing interest in Alice, but a keen devotion—when the American watches Alice in the Roxas living room, and then escorts her to her afternoon siesta, when he bends to hear her every word, I feel an old dread I haven't felt since before the liberation. I, Salvacion Feria, for whom the world has continued even after one revolution and two world wars, now feel the world lurch suddenly and stop. I am not a fearful woman, and yet I have never been so afraid in my life.

* * *

In the dream, he keeps the apple warm in Alice's kerchief. He tells Sawyer there's no need to delay the inevitable; it is time to face his mother like a man. He squares his shoulders the same way he has squared his shoulders in the man-making millisecond before he's had to face his father, or a commanding officer to own up to an offense. He brushes back his hair, and clears his throat as though to cough the courage back in his gut—nothing has made him so fearful as having to face his mother like a man.

In the dream, Sawyer is so lit, he can hardly start Burt's father's jalopy. It would have been a feat even while sober to start this old, broken-down thing. Sawyer is taking what feels like hours to Burt; the longer he takes starting up the car, the less resolved Burt feels to face his mother. In the dream the sun is high but Burt feels cold.

At last, Sawyer starts the car, but as soon as they've gone on that first minute homeward, Burt know things aren't right. He is going too recklessly and too fast. 'Woah, slow down Sawyer,' he hears himself say.

But Sawyer is not slowing down, not any time soon. 'I thought you wanted to see your mama, Burt. Francis says you have quite a bit of news to tell her,' he says. 'What's the news, Burt?' And as soon as he utters the words, he knows that Francis has betrayed his brother to tell Sawyer the truth—that Burt has married a Filipina bride, that she is carrying his half American child, that he is on his way to his mother who hasn't answered any of his letters for the better part of two years, to tell her to get with it. That she must bear the news—if not gladly then tolerably well—or else she will lose him.

But as the liquor settles in more comfortably in Sawyer's blood, he grows more reckless and more belligerent. 'Couldn't keep it in your pants, could you, Burt?' he says, 'Couldn't have married one of the local girls instead; you had to go on and break your mother's heart, didn't you?'

It's taken a good amount of liquor to settle into his system for Sawyer to show him who he is: a common farm boy. If Burt had seen him as an ally a short while ago, he sees him as a belligerent and dangerous enemy now. In the dream, Burt feels like he should sock him in the eye, or bloody his nose or beat him badly, but Sawyer is drunk and behind wheel. Sawyer is everything this town is—he is a white man who believes all other races are cattle or easy.

Burt knows it will not do him any good to argue his case with Sawyer. It will not do any good to tell him everything he has written his mother and Francis about his wife's education and pedigree. Anything Burt may lead with to convince him will be wasted breath and wasted spit.

They are almost on the farmstead when Burt feels a terrible rush of blood to his ears. It was a sensation he had only felt on a Manila battlefield where he had to kill or be killed. Sawyer, he sees, has a rabid, wild look in his eyes. As much as Burt wants to kill him, he wants to kill Burt. He is so red in the eyes that he does not see the block of granite ahead, gray and hot. Burt sees it, and tells Sawyer to go slow. Sawyer only presses his foot on the accelerator. He is going fast, and then faster. Already Burt can see the accident before it happens.

He, She

He tells her no one can get whiter than himself and his forebears, that family lore has it that they had arrived on Plymouth rock; he tells her that his family might sound like aristocracy to her but these stories did not mean anything to him while he was growing up and hearing the old stories. He tells her he has always known exactly who he is: a boy from Deerfield.

She tells him that she has had more than her fair share of grief in this life, that one can conceivably sacrifice husbands to the war but that it is quite a different grief altogether to sacrifice a child. She tells him that she had named her boy Bayani, hero, but had called him also her little Moses, floated along a river in a basket to find his way to her. He'd had to drift, she says, from being unwanted to being wanted, and that his joy had been years in the making.

He tells her that his mother had wanted him to marry Peggy Higgins, the daughter of Mrs Higgins, his fourth-grade history teacher, who did not want him to marry Peggy; who had told his mama he was not a usual boy—but of course his mama already knew this. She had told his mama that he had a sensitivity about him that did not bode well for him. Mrs Higgins had urged his mama to please let him be more accustomed to farm life, seeing as he might be too soft. His mother had listened to her advice and had let him wrestle with his brother Francis a little too hard; she'd let the other boys pelt rocks at him, and him pelt rocks at them, until they couldn't tell who shed more tears come dinnertime, given the pain of sundry nicks and rents in their skin, and the occasional bloody nose.

He tells her, don't get me wrong, I could hold my own, but try explaining this to mama, who'd just had an educated lady—such as Mrs Higgins was—tell her what was wrong about her boy.

His mama had had a spare education compared to Mrs Higgins, and this had made Mrs Higgins words Gospel. She was prepared, his Mama was, to forego all that she knew of him: that he could climb the apple trees better than Francis when he was five; that he gave a boy his first black eye the summer he turned seven. He knew how to take care of himself. Didn't mean he didn't know what was wrong with the world. Didn't mean a soft heart—as Mrs Higgins had apprised his—didn't know how to throw punches when punches were merited.

She says it is not fifty years since American and Filipino intermarriages were considered taboo here. Not just taboo, but a sin even. She says that it was his political forebears who wrought these rules. Americans before him fancied themselves as civilizing lords—but as educated lords, she cannot fathom how they could have thought it was beneath them to marry well in these parts.

He says he can't imagine how the Europeans would have felt, 'civilizing' and inter-marrying with the natives not far from these parts. He says he can't imagine that colonial people like the French in Vietnam, or the Dutch in Java, thought it beneath them to marry the local girls. Or perhaps they did, he doesn't know. It's only really thanks to Mrs Higgins, his history teacher in middle school that he even knew that the French colonized Vietnam, or the Dutch colonized Java. Still: did they look upon the rich, local girls as poorly as Americans look down at these debutantes from good families here in Manila?

She says, I'm glad Mrs Higgins thought you weren't good enough to marry her daughter.

He laughs, says, me too, says, so what do I with you, Alice Feria.

Sunday Times Magazine: 9 May 1945

VICTORY CONCERT SWEEPS MANILA!

By Juan Quijano

A post-liberation concert has just taken place in the ruins of the old Santa Cruz church in Manila under conductor Dr Herbert Zipper. Dr Zipper has come out of his Manila exile to gather the old Manila Symphony Orchestra and perform one more time to a glad Filipino audience. This is the first post-war appearance not just of Zipper, but also of the orchestra, who had briefly disassembled during the war. In their stead rose the New Philippines Symphony Orchestra, that had played quite different concertos, from both Japanese and Filipino playbooks.

Zipper tells this reporter that he had long wanted to play something heroic—not just for the Filipino people who have long suffered under two long occupations and just this brief Japanese one. He wanted the orchestra to play something thunderous and awesome to reflect both world affairs, and not just timely Filipino ones. He had settled, thenceforth, on *Beethoven's Symphony No. 3*, or 'Eroica' to a more formal, discerning public. 'I wanted something to reflect not just our victory in the war, but also our victory over the Nazis,' Dr Zipper says.

Here in the veritable ruins of the old Santa Cruz Church—roof blasted off, sides nicked and grazed by sundry bullets. Santa Cruz, no doubt the proud, staunch witness to sundry war horrors that have just taken place—one today hears strains of Beethoven, even amid the thundering of guns and bombs in the not too far Antipolo hills.

One cannot help but feel that Zipper's choice of music is heavy with symbolism. First extravagant and heroic, *Eroica* then lunges in the second movement into a kind of funereal march. It seems to be a song of mourning for all the lives lost in the war. The piece then launches into heroic climaxes, which must mean how good has finally triumphed over evil. For Zipper this is both a personal victory and a victory for all mankind.

'I was myself in two concentration camps during the war,' he says, 'first Dachau and then Buchenwald. And it is only through the nimblest kind of luck that I survived.'

Asked what he means by this, Zipper answers: 'I got off because my father had petitioned to the Nazis on my behalf, and they had freed me because he had caught them only in the beginning of the war—just when they had started to forget their humanity; they had not yet forgotten all of it.'

Zipper went on to the Philippines to conduct the Manila Symphony Orchestra when their previous conductor had died. 'I knew Lehman, and had mourned his loss as a brother. I felt it was my duty to pick up where he left off in Manila,' he says.

Lehman then brought much culture and cheer to the Manila Symphony Orchestra who had suffered the loss of their conductor, and who had been cast, quite headlong into a new occupation. Famously, Zipper had not wanted his orchestra to play for the Japanese occupation and so the Manila Symphony

Orchestra had been in retirement from the years 1941-45 under Zipper's watch. This retirement had been in place when Pearl Harbor had infamously happened in December 1941. 'The Japs had wanted the orchestra to play their propaganda songs for the Filipino public under their watch,' Zipper says. 'But I would have none of it—it would not happen with my orchestra, and not under my watch.'

Asked if he had learned to love the Philippines during his stint here, he says: 'I have seen many parallelisms between my fellow Jews and now my fellow Filipinos. We are just the same: a persecuted race, even in the places we have wanted to call home. In the years I have spent here, my Jewish predicament has not seemed all too far removed from the Filipino predicament. In this way, I have been able to see Manileños not as strangers, but as old familiars. I have walked past many a Manileño in the streets, and have seen my old sadness in his eyes.'

And there you have it: Dr Herbert Zipper might just be an honourary Filipino. 'I have never seen anyone as determined or as committed to the Filipino cause as Dr Zipper,' says Alice Feria-Obordo, a socialite and a war widow. 'For when Dr Zipper talks about rising from the ashes of the old occupation, I get the sense that he isn't just talking about world affairs, he is talking also of Filipino ones.'

And so we see, well into the sweltering heat of a postwar Manila afternoon, amid a bombed-out church that has seen far better days, and far better imperial times, Filipinos from all walks of life come and hear Zipper's orchestra play. They have come from Malate and Ermita. They have come from Tondo and Binondo, they have come from Santa Cruz, and even as far as Mandaluyong, and Antipolo, to hear Zipper's orchestra play Beethoven's *Eroica*, which is both dirge and heroic song.

'No other orchestra I have conducted has played this piece so unusually,' Dr Zipper says. 'No other orchestra has seemed so determined to keep their spirits alive with only a bit of heroic music. Long live the Manila Symphony Orchestra,' he says.

And here I echo his very words. Long live the Manila Symphony Orchestra, and long live the Philippines.

Epilogue

Alice Feria had warm hazel eyes, and a complexion so white you could see the blue-green veins popping out of her neck excitedly when she told the story of a burning house. I did not hear this from Alice herself. Alice, herself, died at fifty-six in 1979, before I was born. The burning house was her conjugal house in Malate, a district in Manila—a house she shared with her first husband, Ding Obordo, just before the war broke out. It was a house she and her husband also shared with an adopted child she named *Bayani*—or, to those of us our mothers didn't pass the word on to—*hero*.

Alice Feria believed in heroes. She had been weaned on stories of Jose Rizal, national hero. In his time, he was a reformist and author and doctor. History would magnify his status as a burning hero, but he was no revolutionary—any evidence to the contrary can only be speculative. She had also been weaned on stories of the Katipunan, a secret society composed of revolutionaries who had been inspired by Rizal's subversive novels. Through them, Rizal had denounced the injustices Filipinos had suffered under its first colonial master: the confiscation of land from the ordinary Filipino, for example, or the massive retributions delivered to locals by any incarnation of Spanish colonial power—whether priest or governor. Rizal, through his literary work, had dared speak truth to power—to coin a modern phrase.

Alice had been told stories about the Katipunan and the great Philippine revolution of 1896—an uprising waged against Spanish colonial masters. Spain and America perhaps knew these only as pockets of subversion when Spain ceded the Philippines to America in 1898.

At any rate, and anyway, Alice heard the stories, as we all had who came after her—the difference being that Alice was born in 1922, not thirty years after the revolution. Stories of heroes were still as fresh to Alice as perhaps your first heartbreak at seventeen.

Suffice it to say that Alice survived the war—not unscathed, and not completely whole either. She carried its wounds well into her adulthood, and she bore its remnants all her life. She showed a great sensitivity that manifested itself in her love for books and music—but as far as grit went, Alice had her own version of gumption that did not translate obviously to all the strong women in her life, to say nothing of its men.

As one of the first women journalists in the Philippines, Alice's life goes largely unrecorded. Much recorded, however, are the lives of her contemporaries and friends. Alice's circle included distinguished women writers and eventual members of government—this is more than testimony to the Filipina's grit and perseverance at a time when the Philippines had just granted its women the vote, and when its own history depended on the whims of its male leaders and their negotiations with its colonial masters.

Sometime after the war, Alice had birthed my mother, and had lived long enough to witness the births and young lives of my older siblings. She did not live long enough to witness my birth. All I know of Alice I've heard from second-hand stories—fragments of which have been lengthened here into creative fact. What we have here is a literary biography gleaned from stories that have morphed into many versions over the years, and from the memories of a variety of sources.

Growing up, all I knew of Alice were black and white photos scattered that way and this in a pink carry-on with a white handle, and a portrait done when she was thirty-six years old, which still hangs in my mother's home. In the portrait, she is the oldest thirty-six-year-old I know, having survived the American occupation and the second world war. She wears a sleeveless white dress, festooned with a spray of diamonds in its cleavage. Her light brown hair is shorn in a curly bob, much like a Hollywood actress in the 1950s.

In this portrait, you cannot tell by her light brown eyes, and her gracious demeanour, that she has had her share of loss and tragedy. Rumour has it that Manila society had called one of her closest friends the 'dying swan.' As one for whom life was one long aria and one long sigh, the term could have described Alice herself.

For much of my life, Alice has been the other—wholly unknown, and wholly mythologized. That perhaps is the role of the other in any writer's life—a being to be missed and pined for; one that cannot ever be known or touched. The other leaves a crease that can't ever be smoothened out, remains a gap one can never cross, as one would from a train to its station.

This may prove infelicitous to a granddaughter who has never met her grandmother; but as a writer, this is an inspired lack. For I can imagine Alice and see her not through my own eyes, but through stories that have been told and re-told over the years. In this way, I can never fully humanize Alice, no matter how human she seems in the stories that have followed her, even decades after her death. This is not a setback, at least creatively.

As a child, I had perused the contents of that pink carry-on with the ardour of a fangirl. There were the pictures of Alice's youth, but also of Alice in middle age. There were her laughing photos as a young girl, decked out in the fashion of the time, but there too were pictures of her in shapeless caftans during the birthdays and baptisms of my older siblings. I matched the photos to their accompanying stories and followed her life as best I could, given the gaps in the storytelling.

That pink carry-on with its geometric, plastic handle, was lost in a flood in the mid-nineties. It had previously been left in an attic with a leaking roof when a storm hit the city. The photos thereafter remained stuck to each other; those sundered from their paper yielded faces rendered blank and faceless from their tearing. Floodwater had stuck all the photos together into a single, amorphous stack. All the passages of Alice's life had been stuck together, haphazardly, into a single, indeterminate pile by water and forgetfulness.

No longer available to me were pictures of Alice, from the age of sixteen to her days as a 'dying swan'. Here was a life one could no longer enter from the perspective of history; here, instead was a life one could only imagine, given the many stories that have been passed on, over the years, from one generation to the next. The factual had instead been replaced by the oral, and despite its many re-imaginings, and despite the facts that have morphed that way and this over the years, I would like to believe that the essential things about Alice remain the same.

It is those very gaps that I aim to flesh out in the following literary biography. This work has been peopled by characters alleged to have crossed Alice's life—from the time of her birth, to her eventual demise in 1979.

As in a play, the characters are fleshed out as actual people. Through their eyes, one can see Alice, or almost see Alice. Like characters, they are given their own intentions and prisms, and biases and involvements, but one thing remains true: the major characters had loved Alice in his or her own way; each of these characters had at some point saved Alice, either from herself or from the countless perils that plagued Manila when Alice was a young woman in the 1940s.

I owe this literary biography to the pink luggage I lost in the nineties, which would have gladly answered any question I may have had about a grandmother I had never met. In such a loss, I have had to reconstruct the old stories into what I can only hope is an almost rational and cohesive account of her life. With the anecdotes, I have also consulted history books—actual historic timelines have informed happenings (whether oral or factual) in my recounting of Alice's life.

You might ask why a granddaughter would feel so compelled to tell a grandmother's story?

One feels compelled to tell it for a variety of reasons: Alice was born between the old world and the new, during the time the Spanish occupation had led to the American one. In her life as a journalism student, up to the time she had become a journalist in the early 1950s, Alice had been concerned with one project, and one project only: nation-building. She had asked herself and her small audience what could become of the Philippines after its total devastation. She had made this her project when she published a magazine called *The Filipino Home Companion* in the late '50s—she had asked her audience (the youth among them)—what it might mean to be a true Filipino, following two colonial occupations and two world wars.

The glossy also published political and literary work by Eugenia Apostol and Letty Jimenez-Magsanoc (Apostol and Magsanoc would play pivotal roles, in subsequent magazines, in the overthrow of Ferdinand Marcos). Alice did not go on to be a media giant, but to think that fostered and encouraged the next generation of women journalists who began speaking truth to power in Marcos-era Philippines, would not be an overreach.

Whatever answers became available to her, at that time, I will never know. But here and now, when press freedom has been quelled in the Philippines, and women journalists and politicians who speak truth to power are either put behind bars, or are plotted against—a time rife besides with extrajudicial killings and maritime disputes that challenge the idea of nation, one might once more concern oneself with the notion of nation-building. One might ask oneself who we will be, once the current administration is over.

Should this administration raze our ground to metaphoric rubble and ash (as Manila was once reduced to actual rubble and ash), one should ask what might remain of us that can be salvaged and built on. It might be that we have to create new dreams, yes, but these might only be new dreams now given our current reality; these dreams might also be the very dreams of our grandmothers and grandfathers, and their mothers and fathers.

I know this much: that Alice's dreams are mine. I also know what Alice made of these dreams; what I make of mine remains to be seen.

EDITORIALS FROM *THE FILIPINO HOME COMPANION*

To The Graduate (1960)

By Alicia Feria-Winn

The Filipino First slogan is an old story, but is going to be forever new as long as we are interpreting nationalism. It is going to be forever new as long as we are defining patriotism. It is going to be forever new as long as we are interested in the perfection of our country.

We see this slogan being used in our daily newspapers. We hear it over on radio and television and we ourselves talk about it in our homes, schools, restaurants, cocktail lounges and in our corner sari-sari stores.

It appears to have become the moving force—the determining factor in penetrating our appraisals of each other's worth and motives in the all-out drive for self-realization. Through it we seem to be able to detect our faults and our good points, but it seems also that we tend to discover more defects than virtues. As a result, we overlook the tangible testimonials to the burgeoning within our democratic set-up.

For this reason, it is important to care that this powerful gauge or thermometre of our patriotism is interpreted properly. Otherwise, it is easy to be misled and misused.

To the Filipino graduate facing a strange world with education but no experience, Filipino First should mean first of all that he put to proper use everything he knows that is good.

He must be willing to give a full day's service for a fair day's pay. He must be, within himself, his own first arm of government. Restraining himself from wrongdoing, he must be able, morally, to walk alone—to be lonely for those periods of time when to be right means that he will not be part of a group that does not care that it is wrong. He must keep on learning— for not until we close our eyes in death do we stop seeing; not until the sounds of the earth fade from our ears do we stop hearing; not until our hearts stop beating do we stop feeling and not until we are soulless clay do we stop thinking.

The Filipino who is first in the right way is the Filipino who remembers God and country and puts both before himself.

On National Development (1958)

By Alicia Feria-Winn

Imports rise and exports fall. Newspapers every day worry and criticize our national economy. Newspapers every day urge national development. What does this all mean? Where will it all lead?

The tendency to desire what is foreign is universal. Countries grow and develop partly through imitation, partly through initiative. Comes a time when the call to initiative is loud and compelling. A country emerges as a nation only when it realizes its strengths and faults. The prevalent desire for foreign goods, while it may show appreciation for other cultures and, in a way, prove the need for assimilation, is excusable only as long as it does not become a fetish of the people.

In the Philippines, there is a clamorous and urgent call for initiative. We have the land and the climate for rice, our people work and toil in our rice fields but rather than eat the food drawn from the earth by their love and labour of their hands, they eat rice imported from other places. Our sugar plants grow tall and strong in the fields of Negros and Pampanga; our mills crush the red and yellow stalks but we still need foreign facilities to turn sugar into the refined white we like. Men and women walk Manila streets clothed with a touch of tyranny on their backs. It should be a mark of shame for the stain of enslaved people is on every barong and dress woven in communist China.

Why is national development so important and so significant? While newspapers every day worry and criticize, people at every turn fear the possibility of another war—a third and final war.

Actually, we are luckier now than we have ever been. The last war is not too far behind us to remember many things which would answer us now why we must concern ourselves with national development. It is not enough to talk profoundly of nationalism if it only means being proud of what we are and of what is ours. We have a duty to cultivate, improve on and share what is ours and above all to be our first, best, and staunchest customers.

Those terrible war years we experienced not so long ago gave us an insight into our capacity to be self-sufficient. Emergency and need enabled us to get by with less than what we thought was indispensable and very many of us took the test with an enviable ingenuity.

If we must talk of war, let us do it by all means, but with dearly-earned serenity and equilibrium. Total annihilation does not seem as awesome as the thought of realizing we had been intimidated by cowardice. It is incredible that we do not seem aware of our perennial complaint about our national inadequacies and chronic ills. We could not possibly be, however, or we would surely stop talking and start doing something about them for a change. It is quite obvious that we would like to have an absolute and complete leadership of our country but it is equally obvious that we shirk the responsibilities without which such a leadership would be impossible.

The right steps seem to indicate a pressing and immediate change of attitude, an honest appraisal of values and a more intelligent grasp of what it means to fill Tagaytay air with the aroma of coffee, to seek into the depths of the earth for petroleum and oil, to conserve our forests, to stock our waters with fish, to feed our people and to send to others what our land makes available. Finally, to remember that physical survival is not all. We learned from the last war that an unswerving faith to one's ideals and principles is not in vain and the triumph of Truth is irrefutable.

From the Editor (1959)

By Alicia Feria-Winn

A blessed and happy Easter to all our readers and friends! Every easter brings back the joy of the resurrection and something special besides. For us, this year, comes a beautiful package wrapped in white, glossy paper with a spray of lilies and baby's breath held against white lace held together by a wide velvet lavender ribbon. Inside it are two wishes come true: a closer-to-your heart Filipino Home Companion and the possibility of visiting with you every month which we had long hoped for.

We are very happy about this but we are even happier to be recipients of an even more beautiful package which every Filipino has received this year. It is a lasting gift in the rebirth of our national soul.

Did our national soul ever die? No, but it has been submerged if not lost in our multi-phased efforts to keep up with and adjust to the ever-increasing, never-ending demands of our national growth. During that big, overwhelming sweep of our historical progression, our national soul has had to intermittently appear and disappear from our view. Now, it seems that it will never be lost to us again.

This is evidenced by our rightful awareness for nationalism. Yes, there are many interpretations of the word—the most recent one being Filipino First. Yes, this word has been abused and attacked and it has become a farce. However, this is all part of our development. Through all the distortions, misgivings, selfish and incorrect definitions and applications of this word there is a right way of understanding and practicing nationalism. To find this is our business. We cannot go wrong this time because this awareness in itself is a good head start and a promise.

We seem to get at this enlightenment when we follow that awareness in our daily lives and allow it to direct our thoughts and actions sensibly. We express it in our fight for freedom from all internal and external enslaving influences. Also, in our fight for freedom for ourselves to mature correctly and appreciate to hold in contempt any sly or sugar-coated scheme to turn us into demagogues, bigots, imitators, and fools. We express this in our art—in out painting for instance, which brings out our national temperament at once vivid but not violent; at once clear but polite.

We feel this surge in our desire to go beyond our limited boundaries knowing full well that it is healthy to exchange ideas, knowledge, experiences, opinions with all the other people in the world.

This issue humbly carries with it all these implications. We have a record of the activities of the freedom fighters from Hungary, Latvia and Poland in the personal interview of Mayor Kovago of Budapest by UP Economics Professor Janos Horvath; and the accomplishments of the Art Association of the Philippines under the inspiring leadership of Purita Kalaw Ledesma. Jesus Peralta and Malang-Santos, executive secretary and member of the AAP respectively are responsible for our presentation of the winning entries to the 12th Annual Exhibition held on the premises of the Northern Motors recently; in our personal observations of the Filipino Abroad after ten years in the United States in answer to a request frome Exchange Visitors participants whom we lecture to every other week at the Department of Health. This lecture is part of an orientation program sponsored by the Department of Health under the supervision of Dr Manuel Escudero and Dr Trinidad Gomez. It is on an experimental basis at this point but it appears to be of some definite help to professionals going abroad on the Exchange Visitors Program. Dr Escudero lectures on the psychological aspects of going abroad; Dr Gomez speaks on the medical level and Augusto Resurreccion tells them all about travel. There are guest speakers at every orientation period who are chosen according to the professions represented in each group.

This issue is proud to publish the contributions of Ernie Evora Sioco, to hone we are personally grateful for getting us settled in our new printing home; of our new TEENLIFE editor, Marichu Vera Perez who is well loved by people of all ages and all walks of life whom she also loves and our new movie columnist the FAMAS Best Actress awardee this year, Rita Gomez. For a most satisfactory round up we have Jose (Pitoy) Moreno share with us his most outstanding creations this year. Mention of coutourier-designer Moreno inevitably includes the thought of all the other local couturier and designers who together with Manuel Cuenca their PRO-man are helping our local products receive a wider acceptance in our wardrobes and in the fashion world abroad. May this issue be one of the special Easter packages your way.

From the Editor (1959)

By Alicia Feria Winn

Why do we go around shouting about nationalism as if we were not capable of it? As if it was something new that we had discovered?

Why are we blind to our local set-up, for instance to the glaring fact that most of our stores and business houses have foreign names? Our streets, too? Even the motels which seem to be the most enterprising of all our money-making ventures?

Why is it we must sugar-coat our words in dealing with one another? We are like children who must take our castor oil with sugar. We know we are being fooled but we like it that way. We should have found out by now that if we did not teach a child to take medicine with sugar, he would have taken it just the same. We should have also found out by now the effect of the purgative is the same with or without sugar and that the sweet did not make it easier to swallow the oil. Perhaps, we should try sincerity and courage for a change.

We are usually much too sensitive for our own good and usually about things that should not offend us. We do have an inverted sense of values. There is no other way of saying this.

We who have become so used to immodesty around us are prudish let us say about a beautiful act as having children watch their mothers breast-feed the baby of the family.

Our world of entertainment is infested with sex and murder. I would like to know why is there a prevalence of third-rate movies and third-rate everything foreign? Would this be an indication of meekness borne of ignorance or pressure from somewhere? But is this possible of the valiant Filipino—not to know or want to know any better? Is it possible he will accept trash or can he really not distinguish the difference?

Look at our streets. Most of them have foreign names of absolutely no value to anyone. Why California or Pennsylvania (the street I live on) and why Colorado and Broadway. It is a good thing we have already changed Park Avenue.

Go around a little bit and see more of this servile acceptance which drowns any and all national fervor. Most of our shops have foreign names and some of them are grammatically incorrect. It is painful to see an elaborate sign in incorrect French—the people who own the shop must know what a horrible joke they are playing on themselves. These blunders tell on us as a people.

New York is by far more diversified than Manila but there is hardly any attempt to glamorize their shops with foreign names. Those that have foreign names, for instance, the French restaurants, are owned by French people and actually serve French cuisine. Here in Manila, the stores with foreign names are almost always owned by Filipinos. Anyway, the most arresting of these stores is the one somewhere in the northern part of Manila. Boldly perched on a corner is the word PANGIAO. This one, as I said, did not make me laugh.

Just think that in ten to twenty years, if we are not careful, Manila will look like a suitcase of a newly-rich, all worn and patched out with stickers indicating all the countries and all the places in those countries he has visited!

Walk down Escolta and Rizal Avenue or a big office or a construction site and see for yourself the truth of the observation of visiting foreigners: that the Filipino man does not respect the Filipino woman.

When we speak of Filipino First, do we perhaps not mean Good Filipino first? In line with the question of nationalism what exactly do we wish to concretely give the person who will represent our country abroad: a Filipino dress? Excerpts of the Bayanihan? Do we wish him to sing the National Anthem in Tagalog or carry a pocket book edition (there is none so far) of the works of Garcia Villa? Are we perhaps in the process of finding out?

Sources

Luning B. Ira and Isagani Medina, *Streets of Manila* (GCF Books, 1977).

Theresa Kaminski, *Angels of the Underground* (Oxford: Oxford University Press, 2016).

Mark Rice, *Dean Worcester's Fantasy Islands Photography, Film and the Colonial Philippines* (University of Michigan Press, 2014).

Stanley Karnow, *In Our Image: America's Empire in the Philippines* (Random House, Inc. 1989).

Rino D.A. Fernandez, *Diksiyonaryong Biswal ng Arkitekturang Filipino* (University of Santo Tomas Publishing House, 2015).

Nick Joaquin, *Portrait of the Artist as Filipino* (MCS Enterprise, Inc., 2006).

Nick Joaquin, *Portrait of the Artist as Filipino* (MCS Enterprise, Inc., 1966).

Carmen Guerrero-Nakpil, *Myself, Elsewhere* (Circe Communications, Inc., 2006).

Gemino H. Abad, ed. *The Likhaan Anthology of Philippine Literature in English from 1900 to the Present* (UP Press, 2002).

Ay Kalisud, Ilonggo Folk Song.

Terry Sanders, *Never Give Up: The 20th Century Odyssey of Herbert Zipper* (American Film Foundation, 1995).

Margaret Mitchell, *Gone With the Wind* (Sribner, 2011).

Newspaper Articles

Edmund Silvestre, 'All set for the Filipino of PHL's first historical sports drama' (*Philippine Star*, Nov 4, 2018).

Benito Legarda, 'Historic 1945 Manila Orchestra concert to be reenacted' (Lifestyle.INQ, Net March 9, 2015).

Alicia Feria-Winn, 'Editorials from The Filipino Home Companion' (The Golden Age Publications, Inc., 1959-60).

Photograph References

A Clearing Ready for Burning is the name of a photograph found in the Field Museum of Natural History. The full title is *A Clearing Ready for Burning, Limbayao*. 1920.

Bontoc Igorot, *Girl Type 13*. Full length front view, nude. By Dean Worcester (Manila, 1904).

Poetry Extracts and Translations

Rainer Maria Rilke, *The Archaic Torso of Apollo*, Trans. Stephen Mitchell.

Matsuo Bashō, *Quietly, Quietly*, Trans. Makoto Ueda.

Journal References

Christopher John Salamat, 'Resistance, Assimilation and the Building of the Filipino Republic: Architecture of Arcadio and Juan Arellano by Christopher John Salamat' (Thesis submitted to the College of Humanities, California State University, Fresno, May 2013).

Nakano Satoshi, 'Methods to Avoid Speaking the Unspeakable: Carmen Guerrero-Nakpil, The Death of Manila, and Post-World War II Filipino Memory and Mourning' (*Hitotsubashi Journal of Social Studies*, 2017).